C000235031

GARDENING WITH Camellias

Happy Christmas
Ingrid.
love from
Michael, Margaret, Christopher,
Caroline and Jonathan
xxxxx.

Christmas 1992.

GARDENING WITH Camellias

A NEW ZEALAND GUIDE

JIM ROLFE

Cover photograph: 'Fimbriata', a medium-sized formal double *C. japonica* bloom with fimbriated or serrated petals. It was brought to England from China in 1816 for Mr Colvil, a Chelsea nurseryman. 'Fimbriata' was found to be a sport of 'Alba Plena', which had been imported in 1792.

Opposite title page: 'Bob Hope', a black-red, semi-double *C. japonica* cultivar raised by Nuccio's Nurseries in the United States.

With the exception of those photographs listed below, all the photographs in this book were taken by Yvonne Cave.
Ron and Pat Macdonald: pages 14 (right), 15, 27 (left) 35, 36, 37, 40, 42, 44, 114.
Jim Hansen: 16 (right), 19 (left), 31 (right), 41, 56 (bottom right), 57 (top left), 59 (left), 61 (left), 62 (right), 71 (left), 79, 82 (left), 91 (bottom left & right), 92 (left), 95 (top right), 99 (right), 100, 104, 108, 116 (right), 117, 120, 125 (right), 127, 130 (left, centre), 137 (centre, right), 138 (centre, right), 144 (right), 145, 148.
John Lesnie: 31 (left), 59 (right), 67 (right), 101.
Alison Lennard: 121.
Rod Bieleski: 131 (centre).

Published by Godwit Press Limited,
44 Ellerton Road, Mount Eden,
Auckland 4, New Zealand

© Jim Rolfe 1992
First published 1992
Printed in Hong Kong

National Library of New Zealand
Cataloguing-in-Publication data

Rolfe, Jim
Gardening with camellias : a New Zealand guide / Jim Rolfe. Auckland, N.Z. : Godwit Press, 1992.
1 v.
ISBN 0-908877-21-8
1. Camellia—New Zealand. 2. Camellia. I. Title.
635.9331660993

Contents

Foreword

Colonel Tom Durrant CBE, DSO, AHRIH

Flowering, as they do, in mid-winter and early spring, camellias occupy a very special place in our gardens. The mild, oceanic climate of this country provides them with what must be optimum conditions for their growth and prosperity, and their development has been substantially promoted and aided by members of the New Zealand Camellia Society, who have not only grown them with vast enthusiasm, but have done their best to share them with the gardening public at large. During the last thirty years there has been such an amazing increase, both in the number of wild species discovered and the garden cultivars produced, that a bewildering choice of varieties is now available to those who are contemplating the planting of their first camellias.

I know of no one in New Zealand more capable than Jim Rolfe of producing a comprehensive and authoritative study of the genus, which will meet the needs of both expert growers and beginners. He has many years experience as a successful grower and propagator; has read widely in the literature; and had the invaluable experience of editing the New Zealand Camellia Society's publications for six years. He has also travelled widely in many countries where camellias are grown and, while his book is, of necessity, substantially written around New Zealand conditions, the text takes full account of variations likely to be met elsewhere.

Gardening with Camellias covers the history and development of the genus across the world and gives detailed attention to the 'how to do it' requirements of the amateur gardener, aided by very clear line drawings and diagrams. Gardening books frequently stand or fall on the quality of their illustrations. Jim Rolfe has had the advantage of the assistance of several leading flower photographers, who are also experienced camellia growers, and the pictures add to the charm and usefulness of this book. It will be greatly enjoyed by many thousands of dedicated growers around the world, and be a valuable aid to everyone now growing their first examples of the great genus *Camellia*.

Introduction

Camellias were honoured in China during the Ming Dynasty as the 'most beautiful flower under the heavens'. For centuries in Japan they have been an integral part of everyday life. Some two hundred years ago their charm spread to the Western world to captivate admirers in many countries.

My own love affair with camellias began about thirty years ago with the gift from a friend of a very pale pink 'Virgin's Blush'. It gathered momentum after I visited a national camellia show and became a member of the New Zealand Camellia Society. Joining other national societies, reading their literature, and sharing ideas and information with other enthusiasts throughout New Zealand and in places as diverse as the United States, Britain, the Channel Islands, Spain, Portugal, France and China has kept me devoted to this remarkable genus.

From the tea we drink to the ornamental trees and shrubs in our gardens and parks, the camellia is a valued and important plant. This has been recognised by the many countries that have issued postage stamps honouring the genus. Portuguese India began this practice in 1898 and has been followed by Japan, China, Albania, Belgium, Haiti, Korea, Vietnam, Poland, Rwanda, the United States, France and, in 1992, New Zealand.

Gardening with Camellias is an introduction to the genus. As well as giving a botanical and historical overview, it discusses the many and varied uses for camellias in the garden and offers guidance on their care. It aims to give gardeners the knowledge and confidence to widen their horizons in growing camellias and to try new techniques to gain even more pleasure from them.

A garden is a personal thing, and the key to developing an attractive, healthy garden is observation of plants and their reaction to the conditions in which they are growing. Acting on these observations is particularly important with camellias. Do nothing, and they will probably produce reasonable blooms and foliage for many years. Give them some attention and care, and you will be rewarded with trees that are focal points, enhancing your garden at all times—trees that will produce blooms of show quality. They will also be trees of a pleasing shape, size and colour harmony.

Local climate and soil conditions always influence final decisions in gardening. The basic guidelines set out here must be adapted if observations of the local environment dictate it. This becomes increasingly important in

C. japonica 'Wildfire', champion bloom, New Zealand National Camellia Show, 1976, exhibited by the author.

regions that regularly experience either very hot or very cold weather. Camellias are best grown outdoors, and the main text of this book discusses their cultivation outdoors, in the open ground or in containers. However, sometimes climatic conditions or a desire to add another dimension to camellia culture necessitate the provision of permanent shelter. A brief discussion of protection for camellias is outlined in appendix 2.

Growing camellias is a matter of making choices—to spray or not to spray, to prune or not to prune, to disbud or not to disbud. There is not one set formula or programme to be followed for successful growing. Options are set out here, but in the end it is you who makes the decisions, and if you have a procedure that gives you the results you want, it would be foolish to change.

As you become more familiar with camellias and their intriguing range of growth habits, foliage and flower forms, it is likely that you, too, will become addicted and will want to know more about them. The more you understand about camellias, the better you will be able to appreciate and care for them in your own garden.

Growing camellias is a satisfying hobby. If this book encourages you to extend the dimensions of your association with camellias, it will have been worthwhile. Camellias are hardy and easy to care for. Grow them with confidence, and they will repay you handsomely for the care you show them.

Note: Just as this book went to print, Chinese botanists came up with evidence to show that the yellow-flowered camellia *C. chrysantha* should now be known as *C. nitidissima*. This is indicative of the new information steadily becoming available.

Acknowledgements

The support, encouragement and suggestions of many people have been invaluable in the preparation of this book, but if any errors of fact remain, or if any guidelines are not clear, the responsibility is mine and mine alone.

My sincere thanks are extended to:

Colonel Tom Durrant, CBE, DSO, patron of the New Zealand Camellia Society, who has offered many valuable suggestions and, with his wife Bettie, has extended advice and guidance to me over many years; Tom Savige, OAM, of Australia, International Registrar of Camellias, who provided important information on the correct spelling and names of some camellias and checked the text; Mrs Yvonne Cave, FPSNZ, vice-president and registrar, New Zealand Camellia Society, for photographs; Neville Haydon, proprietor of 'Camellia Haven', New Zealand's largest camellia nursery, winner of the 1991 RNZHS Plant Raiser's Award, who has always been prepared to share his extensive knowledge; Jim Hansen, past president of the New Zealand Camellia Society, who supplied photographs and, with his wife Dorothy, advised on the text; Ron and Pat Macdonald, who provided photographs; John Lesnie, professional camellia grower and hybridiser, who provided photographs and whose comments on camellias are always interesting; Professor Emeritus Luther W. Baxter Jnr, of Clemson University, USA, and Betty Hotchkiss, American Camellia Society horticulturist, who provided useful information on the use of systemic insecticides; Sergio Bracci, who, on behalf of the Nomenclature Research Committee of the Southern California Camellia Society, allowed me to use the descriptions in *Camellia Nomenclature*; Les Pinker, who was most helpful with information on bonsai; Roger Anderson, who prepared the line drawings that clarify some procedures; Ann Blair Brown, Executive Officer, American Camellia Society, and Shirley Kilgour, President, New Zealand Camellia Society, who kindly gave me permission to quote extracts from their respective societies' journals; Martin Herbert, tutor in arboriculture, Waikato Polytechnic School of Horticulture, for information on modern care of trees; Dr Rod Bieleski, FRSNZ and Alison Lennard, who also provided photographs.

My thanks are due also to my wife, Heather, and my family, who in many ways have made this book possible. Jane Connor of Godwit Press has also been supportive and helpful.

Camellia nomenclature

Following the convention for botanical nomenclature, species within the genus *Camellia* are printed in italics, for example *Camellia japonica*, *Camellia reticulata*. Naturally occurring variants of species such as subspecies and varieties are written as follows: *Camellia japonica* subsp. *rusticana*, *Camellia pitardii* var. *yunnanica*. (Note: the abbreviation var. is often used incorrectly to denote a variegated colour, in which case it should be spelt out in full, for example 'Guilio Nuccio Variegated'.)

A cultivar (cultivated variety) is a variety that is the result of breeding between two plants and is maintained by cultivation. Cultivar names are always written with an initial capital letter and inside single quotation marks, for example *Camellia japonica* 'Debutante', *Camellia reticulata* 'Captain Rawes'. Throughout this book the terms 'cultivar' and 'variety' are interchangeable for named garden camellias.

Breeding can be intraspecific, between two plants of the same species, or interspecific, between plants of different species. The cultivar resulting from interspecific breeding is known as a hybrid and is identified by 'x', as in *Camellia* x *williamsii* 'Anticipation'. To be classified clearly as the cultivar of a particular species, say *C. japonica*, the cultivar must have a clear lineage within that one species. If there has been any interbreeding between species in an earlier generation or with the immediate parents, a cultivar is considered to be a hybrid.

Botanical practice stipulates that, when designating the parentage of a hybrid, the seed parent (female) is listed first and the pollen parent (male) is listed second. For example, in the hybrid 'Angel Wings' (*C. japonica* 'Dr Tinsley' x *C. saluenensis*), *C. japonica* 'Dr Tinsley' is the seed parent and *C. saluenensis* the pollen parent.

When camellias first came to Western countries, confusion arose over the names and spelling of many cultivars. Camellia societies have attempted to correct many of the inaccuracies, and in most countries the Southern California Camellia Society's triennial publication *Camellia Nomenclature* has been the main reference. Many of the problems that still remain should be eliminated after the 1992 publication of an authoritative register of more than 30,000 species and cultivars, compiled by the International Camellia Society.

When camellias were first imported, names were often changed or lost and later many were incorrectly identified. Often the same cultivar acquired several names. The well-known 'Lady Clare' began as 'Akashi-gata' in Japan but also became known as 'Empress' and 'Nellie Bly'. Following the rules of the International Code of Nomenclature, 'Akashi-gata', the first published name, takes precedence over the others. For the same reason, 'Bokuhan' should be used in preference to 'Tinsie', the name by which another popular cultivar is commonly known.

Japanese cultivar names are generally written as one word—'Akebono', 'Arajishi', 'Oniji'. However, there are a few exceptions. If the name includes a species or group designation, the words are joined by a hyphen, as in 'Shibori-wabisuke', 'Kuro-tsubaki'. In names with adjacent vowels, the pronunciation of both of them is indicated by a hyphen, as in 'Shiro-otome'. Some Japanese names include descriptions like 'shibori' (variegated or striped), 'nishiki' (brocade or pattern), 'beni' (red), 'kuro' (black), 'shiro' (white), 'dai' (large), 'ko' (small), 'shin' (new), 'tsubaki' (camellia). Again, a hyphen is used between the two, as in 'Shiratama-shibori', 'Yamoto-nishiki'. Names that include the character 'no', meaning to, of, in, on or for, are also hyphenated, as in 'Mine-no-yuki' (snow on the mountain peak), 'Toki-no-hagasane' (feather of wild goose), 'Showa-no-sakae' (glory of Showa).

Chinese names have presented their own problems over pronunciation and translation, and most Chinese varieties are commonly known by English names. When transliteration from Chinese characters is used, the official Chinese Pin-yin method should be followed. For example, one popular cultivar should be spelt 'Mudancha' rather than the more frequently used 'Moutancha'.

Today the naming of new cultivars follows strict rules, unlike the situation prior to the 1957 agreement on an international code. Names that existed before then remain and are indicative of practices current at the time. Some of the early cultivars from China and some early seedlings were given Latin names like 'Anemoniflora', 'Alba Plena', 'Myrtifolia' and 'Bronachia'. Under the present rules, Latin is restricted to true botanical names.

CHAPTER 1

The genus Camellia

The name *Camellia* was given to the genus in 1735 by the Swedish botanist and physician Carolus Linnaeus to honour a Jesuit apothecary and naturalist, Georg Josef Kamel. Strangely, Kamel had nothing to do with camellias, although he is known for his association with horticulture when, as a missionary, he described the native plants of the Philippines.

Camellia is one of about 30 genera belonging to the botanical tribe Gordonieae, within the family Theaceae. The genera in the tribe Gordonieae are characterised by the formation of seeds within a capsule. Along with *Camellia*, a number of other genera in the group are used in ornamental horticulture. Perhaps the best known are *Cleyera* (from Japan), known there since ancient times as 'Sakakia', *Eurya* (Japan), *Franklinia* (North America), *Gordonia* (Asia and North America), *Schima* (India to Vietnam) and *Stewartia* (Asia and North America).

The genus *Camellia* is subdivided into species according to floral and leaf characteristics. For a detailed taxonomy, reference should be made to *Camellias*, by Chang Hung Ta and Bruce Bartholomew, and *A Revision of the Genus Camellia* by J. R. Sealy. Together, these books are the definitive, systematic classification of the genus.

The natural home of the genus *Camellia* is a large area of Southeast Asia, China, Japan, islands in the China Sea, countries from Vietnam to Burma, the Assam province of India, and Nepal. This is a huge area with dramatic variations in climatic conditions. Much of it is in the tropics, but the climate of camellia habitats is often modified by a mountainous environment that provides constant humidity, adequate rainfall and partial shade from other trees. The northernmost boundary of the natural home for the genus, approaching a latitude of 40° N, has a more rigorous climate.

Opposite: The early, free-flowering, *C. hiemalis* 'Showa-no-sakae' will make a brilliant show in the garden, as hedging, espaliered or in a tub.

Camellia species

More than 250 species of the genus have been identified. Most of these are distributed throughout southern China. Ever since the plant was named, botanical exploration in China, Japan and other Asian countries—the homelands of the camellia—has resulted in a steadily increasing number of identified species. As Chinese botanists of the Academia Sinica continue their study and exploration of remote areas, it is likely that other species will be identified, and there will be more exciting discoveries to influence the garden camellias of the future.

Without always realising it, everyone is familiar with one camellia species, *C. sinensis*, the tea plant. It probably originated in China and was taken by humans to India and the western Pacific Islands. Varieties of *C. sinensis* are now grown in many countries. Within them there are differences in growth habit, from shrub to small tree, and in leaf size and shape. The variety usually available to home gardeners, *C. sinensis* var. *sinensis*, has long, narrow, crinkled leaves, tiny white flowers and strong, bushy growth. This is the plant cultivated for the unfermented green tea popular in Japan. The other tea variety, *C. sinensis* var. *assamica*, and its hybrids provide most of the tea drunk throughout the Western world.

The most common ornamental species in cultivation is *C. japonica*. With glossy, green foliage and strong growth, its cultivars are valuable garden

C. sinensis, the camellia species from which the beverage tea is produced. *C. sinensis* is now grown commercially in several countries.

Young leaves being picked for processing on a Chinese tea plantation. Regular picking keeps the plants to a manageable size.

From this simple form of *C. japonica*, growing in the wild, the huge range of *C. japonica* cultivars and hybrids now available has evolved.

plants, attractive even when not in flower. *C. japonica* came to the Western world from China, and more than 20,000 cultivars are now known, with flower colours covering a wide range from an almost black red through shades of pink to white. The remarkable ability of *C. japonica* seedlings to produce wide variations, not only in colour but also in flower form, size, colour and serration of the leaves, and growth habit, has resulted in this huge number of cultivars.

C. japonica grows naturally in woodland between latitudes 15° and 36° N. A subspecies, *C. japonica* subsp. *rusticana*, known as the snow camellia, grows further north and higher up the side of mountain ranges, from 300 to 1000 metres (980–3300 feet), on the island of Honshu. Heavy snowfalls every winter cover the plants but they flower as soon as the spring thaw begins. It has been suggested that the unusual cold-hardiness of this subspecies is 'because the winter snow blanket protects them from the extreme temperatures of the mountain winter' (Tom Durrant, *The Camellia Story*).

C. japonica var. *macrocarpa*, limited originally to the Liu Kiu islands, Okinawa, Kunigami and Nagodake, produces very large seed-capsules, often flushed on one side, and is known as the apple camellia because of the resemblance of the seed-pods to apples.

Higo camellias, a popular form of *C. japonica*, are sometimes mistakenly thought to be a separate species. They are distinguished by their single to semi-double form, with five to eleven petals surrounding a profusion of white, gold, pink or red stamens. The name comes from the Higo geographical area

'Gosho-kagami', one of the Higo style of *C. japonica* cultivars now popular everywhere and used extensively in Japan for bonsai.

'Chang's Temple' or 'Zhangjiacha', a *C. reticulata* cultivar introduced in 1964 from China to Western countries.

of Japan, now known as Kumamoto, where these camellias were developed.

The most spectacular of all camellias in flower is *C. reticulata*. Large, vividly coloured blooms are displayed on strong, open growth, and the long, narrow leaves are often thick, flat and dull green with prominent dark veins. The home of *C. reticulata* is restricted to the Yunnan province of southern China, hence the frequent reference to Yunnan reticulatas. These camellias grow in the wild between 1600 and 2500 metres (5250–8200 feet) altitude. They are sensitive to extreme temperatures and do not grow in areas that experience long periods of sub-zero temperatures or severe heat. However, they will establish easily and grow vigorously when given suitable conditions in cultivation.

C. sasanqua is the autumn- and early winter-flowering species well known to gardeners. There is some confusion about the true origins of the species, but it is believed to have originated in Japan, where it has long been a favourite decorative plant. The wild form is a small, woodland tree with narrow leaves and small, single, strongly scented, white flowers. Cultivars generally have heavier leaves and larger flowers, with colours from white through to bright red and varying in form from single to double. As well as

'Plantation Pink', one of the many *C. sasanqua* varieties that flower freely in autumn and early winter. Some are also fragrant.

C. rosiflora, a miniature-flowered species originally from China, popular as a garden plant and used in hybridising programmes.

their early flowering, the spreading habit and fragrance of many *C. sasanqua* cultivars make them useful garden plants.

C. hiemalis and *C. vernalis* are often classified as separate species but there is some evidence that they are hybrids of *C. japonica* and *C. sasanqua*. Both *C. hiemalis* and *C. vernalis* are early flowering and have similar growth habits to *C. sasanqua*, and they are generally found in garden centres listed as sasanquas.

Two miniature-flowered species—*C. rosiflora* (note that this spelling, on the advice of the International Camellia Registrar, is considered correct rather than the more common *rosaeflora*) and *C. tsaii*—have also been well known to home gardeners for a relatively long time. Both the pink-flowered *C. rosiflora*, originally from China, and the white-flowered *C. tsaii*, with long, narrow, pointed leaves, found originally in China, Burma and Vietnam, make a wonderful sight in bloom.

For nearly sixty years hybridists have been breeding from the species mentioned above and from several others from China in their search for improved cultivars. The usual breeding species include the free-flowering *C. saluenensis*, the fragrant *C. lutchuensis*, the hardy *C. pitardii*, and *C. fraterna*, also free-flowering and usually fragrant.

C. saluenensis, like *C. reticulata*, came originally from the Yunnan province of China. There the wild form, a small tree with narrower leaves than *C. japonica*, grows in scrub and open thickets on dry, stony hillsides, as well as on cliffs and steep, grassy slopes. It can also be found in open scrub by streams, in shady gullies and in mixed forests. The single flowers vary in colour from white and pale pink to deep rose-pink with gold stamens.

C. lutchuensis, from Taiwan and the Japanese islands, has weeping growth with attractive foliage, particularly in spring, when the new leaves are russet coloured. The distinct fragrance from the profusion of small white flowers has made *C. lutchuensis* an important parent in hybridising programmes. In its natural home, it is found in woodland from sea-level to 500 metres (1640 feet).

C. pitardii, an open-branched shrub with rose-coloured to white flowers, is represented by two varieties, var. *pitardii* and var. *yunnanica*, differing slightly in certain botanical features—for example, var. *yunnanica* has bigger leaves and begins to flower a little earlier. *C. pitardii* is widely distributed through southern China in thickets and woodlands, on mountain slopes and in ravines, in both light and dense shade.

C. fraterna is widely distributed through central China, a dense shrub, 1–5 metres (3–16.5 feet) high, in open thickets and in shady ravines on rocky hillsides from 150 to 450 metres (500–1500 feet) altitude. Its foliage is dark green and its small flowers are white but sometimes tinged with lilac.

C. granthamiana, another specimen of interest as a garden plant as well as for breeding, was found originally as an isolated tree growing in the wild

C. saluenensis, often used in hybridising programmes in the search for more cold-resistant plants.

C. lutchuensis, a fragrant species that has been used extensively and successfully in breeding new fragrant cultivars.

C. pitardii, a hardy, free-flowering species, which may have rose-coloured, pink or white flowers and red anthers.

on the colder side of a mountain in the Hong Kong New Territories. Subsequent exploration found other plants, and today it is appreciated for its early-flowering habit and its distinctive, large to very large, single, white flowers opening from buds that appear to be dry and dead. *C. granthamiana* is noted also for its large, leathery leaves with prominent ribs.

More recently other species have been introduced to all camellia-growing countries. These have great potential, not only for landscaping but also for hybridising, and will possibly lead to new colours and enhanced fragrance as well as other desired characteristics. Many species are now chosen for their appeal as garden plants, for growing in containers or hanging baskets, and for bonsai. Several, including *C. transnokoensis*, *C. forrestii* and *C. kissi*, featuring small white flowers and some fragrance, are becoming more common in home gardens.

C. transnokoensis was found growing extensively in the forests of Taiwan at an altitude of 2000–3000 metres (6500–10,000 feet). Its slender, arching branches and mass of clusters of miniature white flowers, opening from decorative pink buds, present a striking picture.

C. forrestii was first recorded growing in four well-separated areas of Yunnan, in thickets and forests on mountain slopes at altitudes of 1500–3000 metres (5000–10,000 feet). It was also found in the Tonkin area of Southeast Asia. *C. forrestii* has exceptionally small leaves and white flowers with distinct fragrance. It sets seed readily and makes an unusual sight covered with very small, bronze-coloured and pear-shaped seed-capsules.

C. kissi is widely distributed from Nepal to China, growing to 13 metres (42 feet) high in evergreen forest or scrub and by streams at altitudes ranging from 1000 to more than 2000 metres (3250–6500 feet). Its most popular feature is its miniature white flowers, which are often fragrant.

C. granthamiana, an endangered species in the wild but widely grown in parks and gardens in several countries.

C. transnokoensis, a species becoming widely grown in home gardens for its mass of tiny white flowers opening from ornamental pink buds.

C. chrysantha, the yellow-flowered species that has raised hopes for breeding camellias with new apricot and orange colours.

A yellow-flowered species, *C. chrysantha*, is a strong-growing plant with striking foliage but requires protection from extremes of either hot or cold weather, and is annoying for its reluctance to flower with any regularity. The latest information indicates that 22 yellow-flowered species and varieties of species, including several from Vietnam, and still more forms, are now known in China. The colours range from light yellow to golden yellow. In general they do not tolerate direct sunlight and in their natural growing areas enjoy a high rainfall and humidity, with temperatures from 23° to 30°C.

The widening of the range of species available, and the hybrids bred from them, adds to the versatility of the genus. The considerable differences in flower size and form, the extended flowering seasons and the differences in foliage and growth habit, as well as varying cold-hardiness, increase the landscaping and hybridising options open to gardeners in many and varied environments.

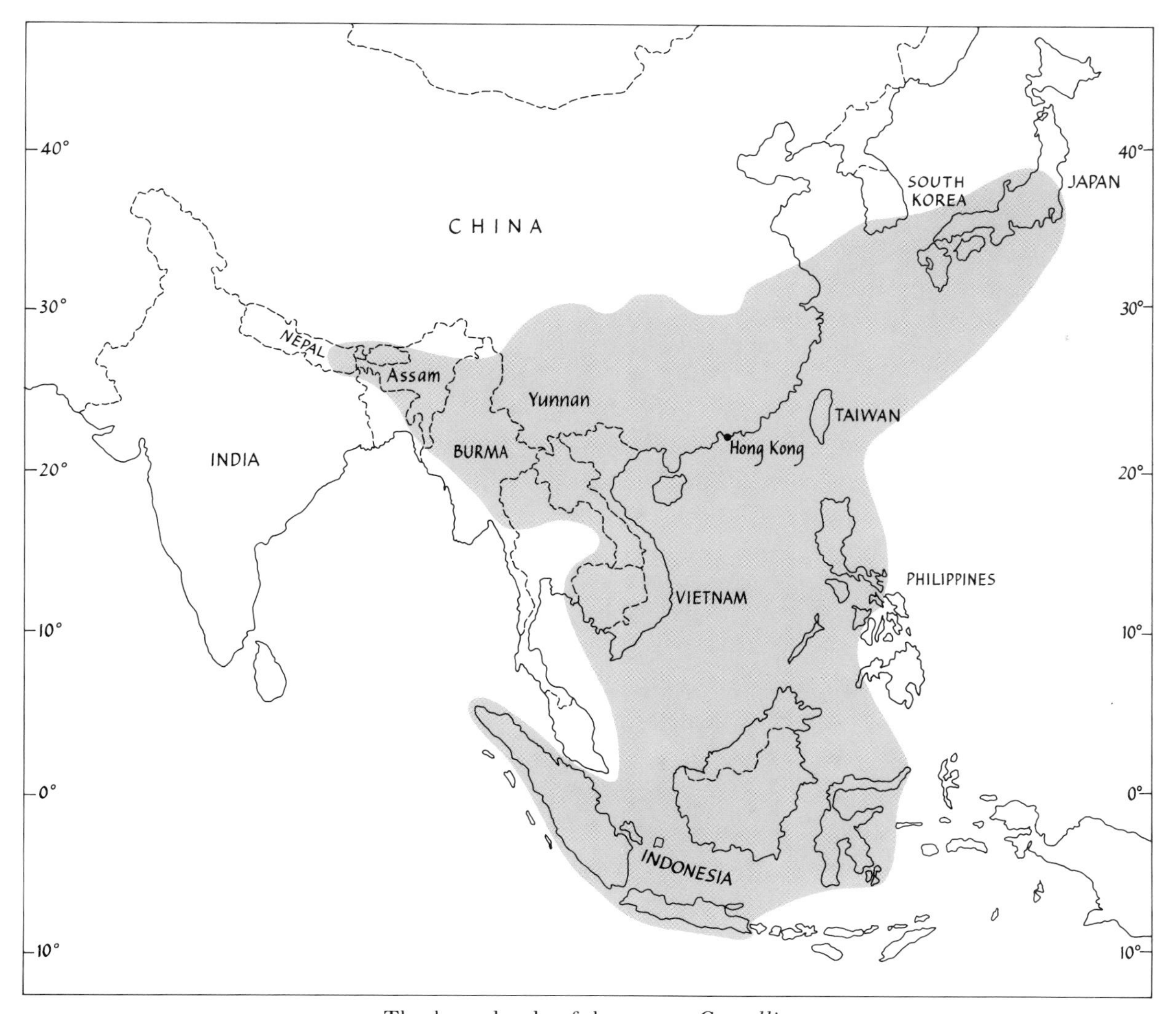

The homelands of the genus *Camellia*.

Camellia cultivars

Some camellia cultivars are the chance result of the activities of bees, other insects or birds. Others are the result of the work of professional or amateur hybridists seeking to enhance the range and quality of available plants. For some hybridists this may be part of a continuing programme to increase fragrance, to develop new colours, to extend flower life or flowering season, to create plants with a preferred growth habit, to increase disease-resistance, or to promote an ability to withstand extremes of weather.

Interest in camellias over the past thirty to forty years has resulted in dramatic progress in the development of cultivars. While basic features of the plant and its flowers have not changed, the blending of attributes from different species has brought a range of varieties with desirable qualities. For example, three camellias raised in the United States and popularly known as 'The Girls'—'Dream Girl', 'Flower Girl' and 'Show Girl'—have *C. sasanqua* 'Narumi-gata' as their seed parent and flower early in typical *C. sasanqua* style, but they also have large flowers derived from their *C. reticulata* parentage—'Buddha' for 'Dream Girl' and 'Cornelian' for the other two.

At first, all new cultivars in the Western world were the result of intra-specific crosses—within the species *C. japonica*. However, as other species became more readily available, interspecific crosses were tried successfully. At first *C. saluenensis* and *C. japonica* were used as parents (see *Camellia* x *williamsii* hybrids, below). The success of these hybridising programmes encouraged experimentation with other species such as *C. cuspidata* and *C. fraterna*. The work of pioneers like J. C. Williams in England, Dr Ackerman, Dr Clifford Parks, David Feathers, J. H. Asper and W. E. Lammerts in the United States, and B. W. Doak and L. E. Jury in New Zealand was an inspiration to other commercial and amateur breeders.

Successful interspecific breeding depends upon the genetic compatibility of the two species. Fertilisation is more likely to occur if plants have the same number of chromosomes. However, there are examples of successful crosses between theoretically incompatible parents. One of the parents of 'Phyl Doak', *C. saluenensis*, has thirty chromosomes, while the other, *C. reticulata* 'Captain Rawes', has forty-five. Extensive studies of chromosome numbers in camellia species have been made so that hybridists today can avoid wasted effort working with species that are unlikely to be compatible.

While a magnificent new cultivar may result from a simple cross-pollination between two plants, often it is a long process involving the hybridist in thorough planning and meticulous record-keeping. It is likely to require back-crossing from a seedling to an original parent and the raising of second- and even third-generation hybrids, always with the aim of

Opposite: 'Dr Clifford Parks', a spectacular ornamental tree and consistent award-winner, raised in the United States by crossing *C. reticulata* 'Crimson Robe' with *C. japonica* 'Kramer's Supreme'.

enhancing desirable characteristics. Camellia enthusiasts with an understanding of basic principles and an appreciation of what has already been achieved can become successful hybridists. Some guidelines for the beginner are set out in chapter 8.

Camellia x *williamsii* hybrids

J. C. Williams in England is recognised as the first successful Western hybridist. His crosses in the 1930s with *C. saluenensis* as seed parent and *C. japonica* as the pollen donor, which brought new flower forms and colours together with attractive growth habits and increased hardiness, were welcomed. Since the first J. C. Williams interspecific breeding success, all *C. saluenensis* x *C. japonica* crosses have been known as *C.* x *williamsii* hybrids. It was the success of this work that gave impetus to hybridising programmes in the United States.

It is significant that the breakthrough was made in England, because there hardiness is a vital attribute for camellias. These hybrids are noted for their ability to withstand frosts and to set a good supply of flower-buds, in spite of restricted sun and warmth, and then to flower freely. It can be claimed

'Donation', a *C.* x *williamsii* hybrid that for fifty years has been one of the most reliable and attractive camellias everywhere.

'Mona Jury', a peony-form *C.* x *williamsii* hybrid, one of many cultivars raised in New Zealand by the late Les Jury.

'E. G. Waterhouse', a *C.* x *williamsii* hybrid, originated in Australia in 1954. A pink, medium-sized formal double, it grows vigorously.

that they are the main reason for the popularity of camellias in Britain today. As well as these attributes, the *C.* x *williamsii* hybrids have smaller leaves than *C. japonica* cultivars and have varying growth habits.

In the following examples of *C.* x *williamsii* hybrids, the name of the *C. japonica* cultivar that provided the pollen placed on *C. saluenensis* is given, together with the name of the raiser and the year of its introduction. Those that originated in England included: 'C. F. Coates' ('Quercifolia', Kew Gardens, 1935); 'Caerhays' ('Lady Clare', J. C. Williams, 1948); 'George Blandford' ('Lady Clare', J. C. Williams, 1958); and 'Jenefer Carlyon' ('C. M. Wilson', G. Carlyon, 1972). With some others, the name of the male parent is not recorded. The most exciting of all these hybrids was 'Donation' (*C. saluenensis* x *C. japonica* 'Donckelaeri'), raised by Colonel Stephenson Clarke in 1941. Around the world, 'Donation' is still considered to be one of the finest garden camellias available.

Not many well-known *C.* x *williamsii* hybrids have originated in the United States but two are particularly worth noting. 'Brigadoon' (*C. saluenensis* x *C. japonica* 'Princess Bacciocchi'), raised in 1960 by Mr Armstrong, is a medium, semi-double coloured rose-pink. It stands adverse weather well and has an open, upright growth habit. The parentage of 'Freedom Bell' is unknown but it has the appearance of a *C.* x *williamsii* hybrid and is assumed to be one. Raised by Nuccio's Nurseries in 1965, it is an outstanding camellia particularly suited to smaller gardens. 'Freedom Bell' has bright red, small, bell-shaped, semi-double flowers displayed freely for a long time.

In Australia Professor E. G. Waterhouse raised a number of *C. saluenensis* x *C. japonica* seedlings to add to the impressive range of these hybrids. The Waterhouse seedlings included 'Bowen Bryant', 'Clarrie Fawcett', 'E. G. Waterhouse', 'Jamie', 'Lady Gowrie' and 'Margaret Waterhouse'. The most commonly grown one of these is 'E. G. Waterhouse' but 'Jamie', as a second-generation *C.* x *williamsii* hybrid, is of special interest for its vivid red colour and medium-sized, semi-double, hose-in-hose form.

Some fine *C.* x *williamsii* hybrids were raised in New Zealand. Les Jury's 'Anticipation' (*C. saluenensis* x *C. japonica* 'Leviathan'), 'Debbie' ('Debutante'), 'Elegant Beauty' ('Elegans'), 'Elsie Jury' ('Pukekura') and 'Mona Jury' ('Betty Sheffield Supreme') have received international acclaim. Many gardeners proclaim the beauty of two *C.* x *williamsii* hybrids—'Water Lily', in spite of inconsistent performance in some districts, and 'Dream Boat'—both raised by Felix Jury using 'K. Sawada' as the *C. japonica* pollen donor.

Breeding for fragrance

For about thirty years the raising of more fragrant camellias has been the goal of some hybridists. Most progress has come from using *C. lutchuensis* as a parent. Other fragrant species include *C. fraterna*, *C. tsaii*, *C. kissi*, *C. sasanqua*, *C. oleifera* and *C. yuhsienensis*, the latter the most recently available and perhaps offering the best promise of real success.

Many cultivars with discernible fragrance are already available. Perhaps the most fragrant of all is 'Odoratissima', which was first raised in Australia in 1866 but is now found growing only in old, established gardens. 'Christmas Daffodil', 'Cinnamon Cindy', 'Fragrant Pink Improved', 'Kingyo-tsubaki', 'Kramers Supreme', 'Scentsation', 'Scentuous', 'Scented Gem' and 'Sugar Dream' are camellias with differing degrees of fragrance readily available today, together with many *C. sasanqua* cultivars.

The degree of success hoped for in developing this much-desired attribute has not yet been achieved. The search began in the USA with people like Dr Ackerman, Dr Clifford Parks and David Feathers devoting tremendous time and patience to crossing *C. japonica* with *C. lutchuensis*, and *C. reticulata* with *C. fraterna*, and seeking to transfer the fragrance of the hybrid 'Apple Blossom' to other hybrids. The late Robert Cutter and the late Kenneth Hallstone similarly became very involved, not only carrying out their own studies and breeding programmes, but also writing extensively and encouraging others to take up the challenge. These two made great progress in their

C. yuhsienensis, a species that has become available recently and is likely to be very important in breeding for more fragrance.

The fragant hybrid 'Sugar Dream', raised by Os Blumhardt of New Zealand using *C. oleifera* pollen on the *C. reticulata* hybrid 'Dream Girl'.

lifetimes, building on the successes achieved by earlier hybridisers.

Some of the newer hybrids raised in Australia and New Zealand have a pleasant fragrance. Ray Garnett of Victoria, in an extensive hybridising programme, and Edgar Sebire have both had notable successes. Jim Finlay, of Whangarei, New Zealand, is one hybridist who has devoted all his efforts to developing a beautiful camellia with pleasant and distinctive fragrance. His hybrids include 'High Fragrance', 'Superscent', 'Katie Lee' and 'Scentuous'. Other New Zealand hybridists to raise fragrant camellias include Os Blumhardt with 'Sugar Dream', John Lesnie with the very slow-growing, weeping 'Quintessence', and Trevor Lennard with 'Gay Sue'.

Extending the colour range

Most camellias exhibit colour within a range from white through various shades of pink and red to the intense, almost black red. Hybridising within these colours has aimed at more striking shades accompanied by improved form and length of flowering. There has always been, however, a great desire to introduce new colours.

Excitement reached a high level when the yellow-flowered *C. chrysantha* was discovered in China. The possibility of a new range of colours including orange and apricot motivated hybridists everywhere, but to date results of breeding from *C. chrysantha* have been disappointing. Interspecific hybridisation using yellow camellias as parent plants began in the Kunming Institute of Botany in China in 1973. Botanists there have access now to a number of yellow-flowered species, and some day, no doubt, there will be success with these breeding programmes. Tadeo Yomaguchi of Ishikawa, Japan, reported in the October 1990 issue of the *International Camellia Journal* of his success in crossing *C. japonica* and *C. chrysantha*. He has named four light yellow-coloured cultivars—'Shoko', 'Ki-no-gozen', 'Kicho' and 'Kiho'.

A true blue-coloured flower has also eluded everyone. It is apparent that the colour of many of the pinks and reds is modified by lilac or purple. 'Persuasion' (purplish red), 'Softly' (soft lavender suffusing to cream in the centre), 'Sally J. Savage' (medium pink shaded lilac), 'Pink Dahlia' (lavender-pink), 'Neil Armstrong' (dull pink with bluish cast), and 'In the Purple' (dark to purplish red with darker veining) are but a few of those cultivars that clearly indicate lavender, lilac, blue or purple in their genetic make-up. There is also the Yunnan reticulata 'Purple Gown'. 'Blue Bird', raised in New

The distinctive flowers of 'Donna Herzilia de Freitas Magalhaes', from Portugal, are often almost purple in colour.

'Wirlinga Princess' sets seed freely, making it potentially outstanding for breeding new varieties.

'Snowdrop', one of the free-flowering miniatures that have become so much admired, is also the parent of some exciting seedlings.

Zealand by Mrs I. Berg, and 'Blueblood' and 'Blue Danube' from the United States are three hybrids with overtones of blue. Perhaps the most recognisable cultivar tending towards purple is the Portuguese 'Donna Herzilia de Freitas Magalhaes'. A few other cultivars are noted for opening as red but turning a shade of purple as they age.

Miniature-flowered and slow-growing cultivars

Fashions change, and as people move into smaller houses with smaller gardens there is a corresponding demand for dwarf or at least very slow-growing camellias. Those with small flowers and matching leaves have a special appeal. Australian and New Zealand plant breeders seem to be leading the way in fulfilling these requirements.

Typical of recent hybridising in Australia is the work of Tom Savige and Edgar Sebire. Tom Savige is credited with the miniature-flowered 'Wirlinga Princess' and 'Wirlinga Gem' (crosses of hybrid 'Tiny Princess' x *C. rosiflora*) as well as 'Wirlinga Belle' (*C. rosiflora* x *C.* x *williamsii* seedling). Also in this series is 'Wirlinga Cascade', a seedling of 'Wirlinga Belle'. The floriferous

Wirlinga camellias, with pink flowers of different forms and spreading or open growth, are attractive garden plants.

Recent Sebire introductions have attracted particular acclaim. 'Sprite' (a *C. pitardii* seedling), 'Snowdrop' (*C. pitardii* x *C. fraterna*) and 'Alpen Glo' (a 'Snowdrop' seedling) are three outstanding cultivars. The free-flowering qualities of each of these varieties will enhance any garden.

In New Zealand there have been many worthwhile achievements. Mrs Bettie Durrant was an early hybridist, raising several slower-growing cultivars using *C. pitardii* as a parent. 'Snippet', 'Prudence', 'Grace Caple' and 'Contemplation', with their larger flowers, are popular garden plants. 'Nicky Crisp' with pale lavender-pink, semi-double flowers, a slow-growing *C. pitardii* seedling like 'Snippet', 'Prudence' and 'Persuasion', is considered by many to be the best of all New Zealand-raised cultivars.

Also in New Zealand, Neville Haydon has made a significant contribution to this search with his introduction of the true dwarf-growing *C. rosiflora* x *C. tsaii* hybrids 'Baby Bear' and 'Baby Willow'. John Lesnie's 'Quintessence', already mentioned for its fragrance, is another important small, slow-growing plant.

Mutants or sports

So far this section has been concerned with the development of new cultivars as a result of pollination, whether indiscriminate or controlled. New features sometimes develop on plants without human intervention or cross-pollination

Two blooms from the same 'Betty Sheffield Supreme' tree; the one on the right has reverted in colour to solid pink.

'Betty's Beauty' has the same beautiful colouring as 'Betty Sheffield Supreme' but is less likely to revert to a solid colour.

Opposite: 'Nicky Crisp' is rarely affected by harsh weather and can be relied on to display many attractive flowers. 'Nicky Crisp' blooms are frequent award-winners.

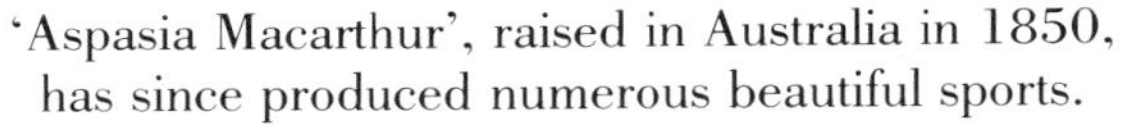

'Aspasia Macarthur', raised in Australia in 1850, has since produced numerous beautiful sports.

'Jean Clere', an 'Aspasia Macarthur' sport first found and propagated in New Zealand.

by insects. *C. japonica* has a propensity to produce unexpected changes in physical characteristics on some parts of a plant. The most common form of these mutants or sports is a colour change in the flower. Another popular sporting characteristic is a change of flower form giving fimbriation of the petal edges, but more common and very attractive is a white-edged flower with a darker centre.

Propagation of the plant stem on which the new flower appears leads to a new cultivar. Unfortunately the stability of the new characteristic is not always certain. 'Betty Sheffield Supreme', for example, is notorious for its instability. At its best, it is a beautiful camellia with white blooms with a deep pink to red border on each petal. However, after a couple of years the blooms may revert to the less-attractive solid pink of 'Betty Sheffield Pink', another form of their common parent, 'Betty Sheffield'. A camellia with similar markings to 'Betty Sheffield Supreme', and one that will not revert readily, is 'Betty's Beauty'.

'Aspasia Macarthur', raised in Australia in 1850, is also noteworthy for producing beautiful cultivars that began as sports. 'Aspasia Macarthur' has medium flowers of peony form, white to cream-coloured with some rose streaks, and over a period of nearly a hundred years has produced several

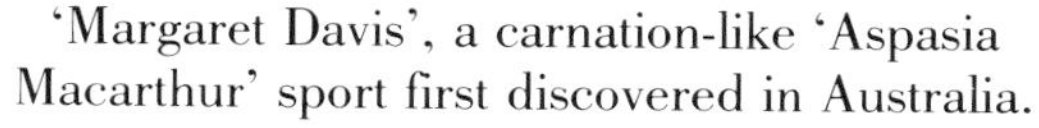

'Margaret Davis', a carnation-like 'Aspasia Macarthur' sport first discovered in Australia.

'Can Can', a sport of 'Lady Loch', a cultivar that originated as a sport of 'Aspasia Macarthur'.

sports that became popular cultivars, for example: 'Lady Loch' (1898), light pink, veined deeper pink, edged white; 'Otahuhu Beauty' (1904), rose-red peony; 'Strawberry Blonde' (1949), light salmon-pink specked deep pink; 'Margaret Davis' (1961), white to cream with rose-red splashes and edged bright rose-red; and 'Jean Clere' (1969), bright rose-red with band of white around petal edge.

The great variation within this 'Aspasia Macarthur' family is increased when sports that first appeared on sports are added. The best-known include: 'Can Can' (1961), pale pink with darker veining and petal edges, which appeared first on 'Lady Loch'; 'Glamour Girl' (1955), light salmon-pink, veined and marked deep pink, on 'Strawberry Blonde'; and 'Just Sue' (1971), light cyclamen-pink edged bright rose, on 'Margaret Davis'. It is intriguing to think that any one of these named varieties may appear at any time on any other plant of the family.

The beautiful and widely grown cultivars 'C. M. Wilson', 'Elegans Splendor', 'Elegans Champagne', 'Elegans Supreme' and 'Hawaii' are all members of the noted and extensive 'Elegans' sporting camellia family. Other common *C. japonica* cultivars that have sported include 'Tomorrow' and 'Donckelaeri'.

CHAPTER 2

Camellias around the world

China

In the book *China's Rare Flowers*, by Wang Jiaxi and Ma Yue, the common camellia is described as 'decorating courtyards, garden paths, rocks and potted landscapes . . . the wood is good carving material, the seeds can be pressed for oil, the leaves are essential in making soft drinks and the flowers are medicinal ingredients'. The writer points out also that since ancient times, the camellia has been known for ten prominent features:

1. It lives up to 400 years without aging;
2. It reaches a height of 50 feet;
3. The bark is rough, yet sleek;
4. The twigs intertwine into the shape of a dragon;
5. The roots curve in the form of grain bins;
6. The large leaves resemble tents;
7. It can tolerate snow and frost, and is green throughout the four seasons;
8. It flowers continuously for two to three months;
9. When kept in a vase, the flowers remain fresh for about two weeks;
10. It is attractive but not flashy.

China has a long history of camellias being used as ornamental plants. Decorative art from the Tang Dynasty (AD 618–907) shows *C. reticulata* cultivated in gardens and Buddhist temples. During the Ming period (AD 1368–1644), *C. reticulata* cultivars were propagated and often used by the wealthy as significant gifts. Even before this, the camellia in its semi-double and double forms had been a subject of decorative art on scrolls, porcelain and inlaid boxes.

Camellias have also been important in providing food, cosmetic, culinary and industrial oils, high-grade charcoal for fuel, and, of course, the beverage tea from *C. sinensis*, which has probably been drunk in China since the third millenium BC. Food was also derived from young green leaves, which were boiled then fermented in holes in the ground lined with plantain leaves and covered with more plantain leaves, earth and heavy stones. After several months, the preserved tea could be used to prepare a drink or, dressed with oil, be eaten as a solid with garlic or dried fish. In southwestern China, tea is prepared in brick form and sent to Tibet, where it is laced with yak butter.

Oil from camellia seeds has long been important. All camellia species contain oil, but through selective breeding the best oil producers are being cultivated. *C. oleifera* was the earliest species used for oil, but *C. chekiangoleosa*, *C. reticulata*, *C. grijsii*, *C. vietnamensis*, *C. crapnelliana* and *C. gauchowensis* are among those being cultivated. Camellia oil is described as being of very high quality and having a long storage life. It is widely used in China and Japan for cosmetics and medicinal purposes.

Camellia cultivars planted hundreds of years ago are still alive today and presenting a vivid mass of colour each year. One of the most common is 'Shizitou' ('Lionhead'). Scientists of the Kunming Institute of Botany have estimated that two specimens in the grounds of a nunnery in Guanzhuang are 600 years old. According to tradition, another cultivar, 'Mayetaohong' ('Reticulate Leaf Crimson'), was planted at the Panlong Monastery in 1347, during the Yuan Dynasty. There are others reputed to be more than 200 years old and many aged at least 100. These remarkable specimens are

The oil-producing species *C. chekiangoleosa*, growing in the Wuhan Botanical Gardens in China.

Oil obtained from camellia seeds has been widely used in China and Japan for cosmetics and medicinal purposes.

Camellias are found growing in the wild in many parts of China. Here a grove of *C. reticulata* camellias is growing near Tenchong.

C. reticulata, of the Yunnan province. The centre of the province is Kunming, known as 'Spring City' because of its all-year-round mild climate. Here the surrounding mountains are covered with wild camellia trees, and in the city there are still many old camellias in temples and gardens.

One of the most interesting camellia collections is that in the Kunming Botanical Garden of the Kunming Institute of Botany, Academia Sinica, whose scientists are world leaders in camellia research. An area of 2.7 hectares (6.5 acres) is set aside for the camellia garden, which includes *C. reticulata* and *C. japonica* cultivars as well as other species. In 1984, an International Camellia Garden of Friendship was established there with cultivars from around the world.

Camellias can also be seen in some small, private and beautifully maintained gardens, as well as in monastery gardens and in places like Mt Emei in western Sichuan. In the mountains between Dali and Kunming, it is possible to see *C. saluenensis* growing naturally, and around the Shanghai area there are many *C. japonica* cultivars.

Because of the mountainous nature of the country and difficulties in transportation and communications, there was limited movement of plant material

An old camellia growing in a courtyard adds colour to the street scene as it hangs over a wall in Tenchong, China.

in ancient times, even within China itself, and it was a long time before different species became known outside their immediate environment. There they grew and hybridised without any formal classification. Chinese scientists have spent many years exploring remote areas, discovering new wild plants and classifying them, while also improving techniques of propagation and cultivation. In recent years western camellia growers and Chinese scientists have exchanged visits, information and plant material, and people like Professors T. T. Yu, Zhang Ao Luo and Feng Guomei, Madam Xia Lifong and Mr Zhu Xianghong, to name but a few, have done much to add to our knowledge. Within China itself contact among growers has increased. In 1988 the first Chinese National Camellia Show was held in the Hangzhou Botanical Gardens. Five thousand potted plants, including more than 500 cultivars, from all over the country were on display.

Japan

Many Western visitors to Japan will have vivid memories of the tea ceremony. This important ritual uses 'green' tea manufactured from *C. sinensis* var.

sinensis in a process in which the fresh green leaves are briefly steamed before being rolled and dried.

Throughout Japanese history the camellia has been culturally significant. Its use, either as a raw material or as a motif, is diverse—textiles, ceramics, brewing, cooking, household utensils, tools, printing, crafts, farming, fuel, medicine, foodstuffs and cosmetics all owe something to the camellia. Camellias are the subject of many paintings and decorations, and camellia plants are used as roadside trees and fences. More than thirty communities have selected it as their symbolic flower.

Japanese people appreciate simple beauty and see it in single to semi-double camellia flowers of the Higo style. In camellia shows, too, this appreciation of uncomplicated beauty is seen in the display of advanced buds or partially opened flowers. The Japanese have also enhanced the camellia's charm in their development of bonsai and ikebana. 'Japanese life does not exist without the camellia,' says Kirino Shuho of the Japan Camellia Society.

Many Japanese parks, botanical gardens and reserves feature camellias, some with extensive collections. The Snow Camellia Garden at Furusawaya has 40,000 plants with 300 varieties of *C. japonica* subsp. *rusticana* (see also page 15). Two other snow camellia gardens in the Niigata Prefecture—Toriyanogata Park and Kamoyama Park—have thousands more plants of this

'Botan-yuki', one of the cultivars of the *C. japonica* subspecies *rusticana*, known as snow camellias for their ability to survive the snows of their home area.

'Tama-no-ura', an excellent example of the single flower form so popular in Japan, where it was raised. It has a vigorous, upright growth habit and flowers in mid-season.

subspecies. The Camellia Garden of Tokyo Municipal Oshima Park is full of *C. japonica*, including 2000 plants of the wild form, while *C. sasanqua*, the city's symbolic flower, is featured in the Kawaguchi Camellia Garden. Numerous other gardens display huge numbers of plants, including many cultivars from other countries. One private garden, belonging to Mr Hiromitsu in Tosa, is of special note, with several plants more than 100 years old included in the 850 plants of 600 domestic varieties and 250 plants from overseas that are featured in his garden.

Co-operation and the sharing of knowledge between camellia enthusiasts of Japan and other countries has been excellent for many years. This has meant that there is a steady and continuing interchange of new cultivars with Japanese growers. Many of those suggested in later chapters were raised in Japan.

As Chinese and Japanese growers continue to exchange visits, sharing knowledge and plant material with Western enthusiasts, breeding programmes and the range of cultivars available will be extended everywhere.

Europe

Camellias first came to the West early in the seventeenth century with the beverage tea, from *C. sinensis*, and it was the demand for the tea plant that led ultimately to interest in ornamental camellias. Many plants arriving in Europe that were supposed to be *C. sinensis* were in fact *C. japonica*. It is not known whether this switch was deliberate or happened because of language difficulties. Whatever the reason, camellias were to become treasured garden plants, particularly when, in 1792, 'Alba Plena', a beautiful white formal double, and 'Variegata', with red and white petals, arrived. A tremendous interest in camellias throughout Europe was generated by these two cultivars.

There are many fascinating stories about the spread of camellias between Japan, China and the rest of the world. In *The Camellia Story*, Tom Durrant quotes Pehr Osbeck, chaplain to a Swedish East India Company ship, who wrote in his diary on 4 January 1752: 'After a stay of four months and ten days in China, our ship and the other Swedish ships began their voyage home. Everyone leaped for joy, and my Tea Shrub, which stood in a pot, fell upon the deck during the firing of cannons, and was thrown overboard without my knowledge, after I had nursed and taken care of it a long while aboard the ship . . .' Some later efforts, after promising beginnings, also failed. Even when some plants were successfully raised from seed planted in containers at the start of the voyage, they did not survive the severe Swedish weather.

English, Dutch and Portuguese traders in the seventeenth and eighteenth centuries, horticulturists and Jesuit missionaries all played a part in bringing camellias to Europe. It is not known for certain who successfully introduced the genus to Europe. There are some very old camellias still surviving in Portugal, but the first record of camellia material to reach Europe was made by James Petiver, an apothecary and botanist of London, who had received dried herbarium specimens collected in China by James Cunninghame late in the seventeenth century.

Tom Savige suggests in *The Camellia* that Jesuit missionaries probably brought the first living camellia plants to Europe, as in 1739 'a semi-double red camellia was reported growing in the glasshouses of Lord Petre at Thorndon Hall in Essex'. Lord Petre, highly esteemed as a botanist and a patron of horticulture, apparently received the plant from China because it was called the Chinese rose.

C. reticulata first arrived in 1820, when a ship's captain, Richard Rawes, brought from China what became known as Captain Rawes' camellia. Another Yunnan *C. reticulata* cultivar to cause a sensation in Britain in the nineteenth century was 'Robert Fortune', honouring the plant explorer who spent many years in China. 'Robert Fortune' is also known as 'Pagoda' or by its Chinese name 'Songzilin'. 'Captain Rawes', a very large carmine-rose-pink semi-double, and 'Robert Fortune', with a large, deep scarlet, formal

The striking beauty of 'Captain Rawes', the first *C. reticulata* cultivar to be brought out of China, is well displayed as it overhangs a garden wall in Jersey, Channel Islands.

'Robert Fortune', often known as 'Pagoda', another early *C. reticulata* cultivar to come from China, brings vivid colour to any garden setting, with many individual blooms of exhibition quality.

to rose-form double flower, are still among the most spectacular of garden camellias.

Camellias gradually became established throughout the continent, and their popularity increased until late in the nineteenth century. 'By the end of the century, garden writers were commenting on camellias still flourishing among the ruins of glasshouses which had fallen down around them and finally camellia flowers virtually disappeared from the social scene. The collapse of interest is sometimes attributed to boredom with the endless proliferation of formal double flowers, all very much alike. This may be partly true, but the real reason was that a social era was coming to an end, and camellias, one of its symbols, joined it in eclipse' (Tom Durrant, *The Camellia Story*).

Before this decline, camellias had been important, not only in England, Holland and Portugal, but in Spain, Belgium, Germany, Italy and Russia. Nurseries and horticulturists had produced thousands of seedlings and made many other imported varieties available to gardeners. Some of the old varieties still grown today are listed in the 1981 historical edition of *Camellia Nomenclature*. Included among them are 'Adrien Lebrun' (Italy, 1885),

The versatility of camellias for landscaping is seen in this avenue of cultivars at Torre de Lama, Spain.

'Alba Casoretti' (Italy, 1844), 'Alba Plena' (China to England, 1792), 'Alba Speciosa' (Belgium, 1849), 'Auguste Delfosse' (France, 1864), 'Augusto L'Gouveia Pinto' (Portugal, 1890), 'Elegans' (England, 1831) and 'Madame Picouline' (Belgium, 1855).

Another important development was the collection of camellia seeds in China by the plant explorer George Forrest from 1917 to 1932. The crossing of *C. saluenensis* with *C. japonica* by J. C. Williams began the line of hybrids now known as *Camellia* x *williamsii* (see page 24), which introduced a new era of outdoor camellia growing in colder climates. Cultivars bred from *C. saluenensis* form flower-buds at lower temperatures, making them the best choice for most of the British Isles, at least.

An appreciation of the camellias of Europe can be gained from visiting some of the famous gardens open to the public—such as Leonardslee, Bodnant, Exbury, Caerhays, Borde Hill, Heaselands, Sheffield Park, Wisley, Windsor and the less well-known Ard-Daraich in Britain. Two areas are set aside for camellias in the Valley Gardens, Windsor Great Park, with hundreds of plants making a fine show. The finest and most reliable display comes from the *C.* x *williamsii* hybrids, but a more varied display of colour and form is presented by the *C. japonica* cultivars. At Bodnant in the north of Wales one bank is planted almost entirely with camellias, which flower freely. This garden is associated with three generations of the Puddle family as head gardener. Charles Puddle, MBE, VMH, father of the present head gardener, is known throughout the world for his contribution to camellia knowledge. Over in southern Ireland, the camellia collection at Mount

Congreve is said to be one of the best in the region. Here there is a wide range of plants, but again it is the hybrids that are particularly successful.

In France, the Botanical Gardens at Nantes (Jardin des Plantes) and Angers have significant camellia collections. It was at Nantes and throughout Brittany in the mid-nineteenth century that it was demonstrated that the camellia could be grown outdoors as well as in the protection of a greenhouse. Henri Guichard of Nantes and his daughters helped improve the appreciation of camellias by exhibiting them at the 1912 Chelsea International Exhibition.

A visit to European camellia gardens should include the Channel Islands; and in Spain too, particularly in Galicia, there are several gardens where very old camellias can be seen alongside the new. An interesting, relatively new garden is La Saleta, near Pontevedra, developed by the late Robert Gimson. And the list goes on. Beautiful gardens in Italy, such as at Villa Taranto and the Villa Anelli, old camellias in Portugal, and camellias in Germany are all examples of the world-wide appreciation of the genus.

It might be expected that considerable efforts would be applied to hybridising throughout Europe in the search for cultivars with increased cold-hardiness. However, compared with the United States, Australia and New Zealand, there are few developments. Britain's leading hybridiser for the last

Camellias feature among ornamental shrubs in the National Trust's Sheffield Park Garden, in East Sussex, England.

thirty years was Gillian Carlyon, owner of Tregrehan in Cornwall. From 1960 until her death a few years ago, she was devoted to the Tregrehan camellia collection and to raising new varieties using *C. saluenensis* and *C. japonica* as parents. 'China Clay', 'E. T. R. Carlyon', 'William Carlyon', 'Gwavas', 'Edward Carlyon' and 'Tregrehan' feature among her many successes.

Though the raising of new varieties is relatively slow in Europe, research proceeds steadily. The work of Dr Jean Creze in France, investigating in vitro cuttings, virus eradication and improved resistance to cold, will have important benefits in the future.

The United States of America

The introduction of camellias to the United States marked the start of an interest that paralleled that in Europe. Surprisingly, in spite of regular sea trade, camellia plants or seed did not reach the United States until the middle of the eighteenth century, though the Dutch had brought processed tea to New York in 1650. Efforts, begun in 1774, to establish tea growing in several states were unsuccessful. It is believed that the first *C. japonica*, a single red, was imported to New Jersey in 1797 or 1798.

From the east and the north, new cultivars spread to gardens in the south and to the west. Philadelphia became a camellia centre about 1840, and

Glasshouses have been important for growing camellias in colder climates. Here they are being cultivated under glass on Long Island, New York.

Two of the many varieties raised by Nuccio's Nurseries in the United States. Left: 'Bob Hope', a black-red, semi-double *C. japonica* cultivar. Right: 'Twilight', a formal double *C. japonica* of a very delicate blush-pink colour.

large collections became common in the southern states. Sacramento was the first city in the West, in 1852, to obtain plants and was named 'Camellia City' in 1910. This was a time of renewed interest, and shipments of camellias came from Japan to the west coast and from Germany, Belgium and France to the east. The enthusiasm of growers led to the establishment of the American Camellia Society as a national organisation in 1945.

Since the Second World War growers in the United States have been very active seeking perfection in blooms. The most enthusiastic growers are often keen, competitive exhibitors as well, which may be the reason why larger blooms retain their popularity over the miniature-flowered varieties now the fashion in New Zealand and Australia. Variegated flowers are also popular, which has caused some controversy as it involves introducing a virus into the plant.

Whatever their preference in flower size or pattern, growers in the United States are responsible for the introduction of outstanding new varieties, popular around the world. Many of these come from Nuccio's Nurseries in California, but there are also many active, amateur hybridists throughout the United States. Some of the Nuccio introductions are readily identified by name—'Nuccio's Ruby', 'Nuccio's Pearl' and 'Nuccio's Jewel'—and others include 'Freedom Bell', 'Silver Cloud' and 'Show Time'. The names of people like Frank Pursel, Howard Asper, Dave Feathers, Meyer Piet and the Kramer brothers will always be associated with cultivars that have given great pleasure to gardeners around the world.

There are numerous public plantings of camellias throughout North America. From the internationally acclaimed Butchart Gardens in British Columbia and the Allan Gardens in Toronto, Canada, through many of the United States and down to Central America, there are camellias to admire. Huntingdon and Descanso in Los Angeles can be the start of an exciting camellia trail to gardens in many states. In Mexico, camellias were spread through the efforts of the Mexico City Garden Club. One family is reported to have 10,000 camellias on their ranch. Guatemala also has thriving camellia plantings. In many places camellias are grown in woodland settings to gain the protection of other trees; in others the intense summer heat calls for shadehouses of various types.

Australia

The first recorded camellias in Australia were brought from England by Alexander Macleay in 1826. The large number of plants included *C. japonica* 'Crassinervis', 'Gloriosa', 'Grandiflora' and 'Coccinea'. Five years later another consignment arrived, this time in a case on the deck of the ship *Sovereign*, for the Macarthurs of Camden Park. One camellia of this 1831 collection, 'Anemoniflora', is still growing at Camden Park.

From those early importations, camellias spread through the Australian colonies. Nurserymen played an important part in the introduction of camellias from Europe to Australia, and names like Thomas Shepherd, Michael Guilfoyle, Silas Sheather, Alexander Hunter, Charles Newman and John Rule figure prominently in the camellia history of New South Wales, Victoria and South Australia. Many varieties raised in the earlier years of Australia's development are still grown today, for example 'Aspasia Macarthur', 'Leviathan', 'Speciosissima', 'Helenor', 'Great Eastern' and 'Prince Frederick William'.

In Australia new seedlings were raised by the Macarthurs and other settlers. Camellia growing in Australia increased steadily if unspectacularly until the 1950s, when a new impetus to promote camellias was provided by Professor E. G. Waterhouse, leading to the formation in 1952 of the Australian and New Zealand Camellia Research Society. (Six years later, when the New Zealand Camellia Society was formed, New Zealand was dropped from the title.) The professor's first efforts, in the 1930s, had been aimed at the identification of unnamed plants in old gardens and cemeteries. Then, for many years, he raised camellias and provided leadership and encouragement to camellia growers, not only in Australia but also inter-

Eryldene, former Sydney garden of the late Professor E. G. Waterhouse, who was active in promoting interest in camellias. The garden is now controlled by a trust.

nationally. His drive and contacts with growers around the world led to the founding of the International Camellia Society in 1962 and his election as its first president. Ever since then, Australia has had camellia leaders, researchers and hybridists assisting other growers, often in difficult environments.

Australia can lay claim to many admired cultivars, such as 'Can Can', 'Lady Loch', 'Polar Bear', 'Plantation Pink', 'Overture', 'Samantha', 'Pavlova', 'Bert Jones', 'Jennifer Susan', 'Exquisite' and 'Lucinda'. It is also the home of two remarkably similar *C. japonica* cultivars featuring centres of pale, primrose petaloids. 'Brushfield's Yellow', raised by Keith Brushfield, and 'Gwenneth Morey', registered three years earlier in 1965 by Dr B. R. Morey, are so similar that in shows they are exhibited together.

As the work of hybridists like Edgar Sebire and Tom Savige continues (see page 29), and their introduction of small-leafed, miniature-flowered varieties is acclaimed, other hybridists set different goals. Dr Terry Pierson sees heat-tolerance as just as important an objective as cold-hardiness and believes that species from Southeast Asia could be effective in this search. Dr Bob Withers,

'Pavlova', a clear bright red, semi-double *C. reticulata*, very large in size.

'Pink Ruffles', a *C. pitardii* hybrid seedling raised by leading hybridist Edgar Sebire.

White guard petals surround the pale primrose-yellow petaloids of 'Brushfield's Yellow'.

'Alpen Glo', a 'Snowdrop' seedling from Edgar Sebire which has quickly become popular.

Four Australian-raised cultivars.

through his hybridising and research into species, is also making an important contribution, along with other growers, to the extensive range of Australian-raised cultivars.

Some fine camellia gardens with extensive collections are open to the public. In Sydney, the E. G. Waterhouse National Camellia Gardens were opened in 1969, a co-operative project between the Camellia Society and the local authority. Another notable garden, 'Eryldene', now controlled by a trust, was the property of the late Professor Waterhouse, who established an extensive and comprehensive camellia collection.

For people in Adelaide, the Stangate Camellia Garden provides an opportunity to see many different varieties in association with other old trees and shrubs. As in other areas, some of the older, camellias are of historical interest. In Victoria, the camellia garden at Olinda serves a similar purpose. In Queensland, historical Ormiston House at Moreton Bay, about 25 kilometres (15.5 miles) from the centre of Brisbane, is surrounded by grounds that include splendid camellia gardens.

New Zealand

For some years the camellia has been, arguably, the most popular ornamental plant in New Zealand. This is understandable considering the ease with which the camellia grows in this favourable environment. Nowhere does the country experience, except perhaps in Central Otago and Southland, the severity of weather common to other camellia-growing countries. Public plantings, from the north of the North Island to the south of the South Island, allow the traveller, as in Australia, to see how well the camellia thrives in a changing environment.

Today camellias are grown extensively, with thousands of new trees being planted in New Zealand gardens every year. While this interest has been gaining momentum since the 1950s, the importance of camellias as ornamental trees can be traced back to the arrival of European settlers in the mid-nineteenth century.

Very large camellia trees are magnificent memorials to the colonists. They may be found growing in farm paddocks, cemeteries, churchyards and reserves. These are striking evidence of the camellia's ability to survive and even flourish with little attention. Sometimes they provide the last remaining evidence of an early homestead garden. Some of these are now more than 150 years old and are typical of the cultivars popular in the nineteenth century. In places like Woodlands at Gordonton, Hamilton, and the Hautapu cemetery at Cambridge, there are magnificent specimens planted in the early days of settlement. They also demonstrate dramatically the size to which these trees may grow if uncontrolled. In Woodlands, for example, *C. japonica* 'Lowii' is estimated to stand a commanding 14 metres high with a spread of 12 metres (46 x 40 feet).

'Contessa Calini', more than 100 years old, among other camellias of similar age in the Hautapu Cemetery, Cambridge, New Zealand.

Although most of these early camellias were brought by settlers of British origin, the first plants coming with missionaries and others from Australia, there are also fine old camellias growing in the South Island at Akaroa, where a small settlement of French colonists was established in 1840. The French influence remains visible today in street names, and also the old camellias, one of which, 'Madame Picouline', is still popular.

There is further evidence of the popularity of camellias in the newspaper reports of the 1880s and 1890s of regular, annual camellia shows. The extent to which camellias were grown then is indicated by scheduled classes for groups of 12, 15, 18 and even 24 blooms. It is evident that growers at this time also appreciated the versatility of the camellia. Show schedules listed several classes for flower arrangements, including bridal, table and hand bouquets, as well as posies and buttonholes. There were even classes for funeral wreaths and crosses.

There is no similar evidence of such strong interest in the first half of this century. However, nurseries continued to offer some camellias for sale, and in the 1930s there were two valuable additions to the varieties available. *C. reticulata* 'Captain Rawes' and *C. japonica* 'Lady Clare', imported by a Whanganui nurseryman, the late Wally Stevens, were exciting newcomers.

Dramatic change came after the Second World War, as it had in Australia. Probably the first indication of future developments was the decision of New Plymouth nurseryman Gordon Adams to join the American Camellia Society and to import large numbers of camellias to start a specialist nursery. Adams' interest had been aroused during military service in Japan.

About the same time, Colonel Tom Durrant and his wife Bettie were becoming established on a Tirau farm after migrating in 1947 from Britain. As with Professor Waterhouse in Australia, the Durrants in New Zealand were to be the catalysts for progressive changes in horticultural interests. It is not an exaggeration to claim that the influence of Tom Durrant was to be significant in every major camellia development in the forty years from 1950. The Durrant garden became a showplace. Several hundred camellias were planted after the entire stock of the Adams' nursery was purchased. The colonel corresponded regularly with camellia experts overseas, obtained all the camellia literature available, and learnt everything he could about the genus. As well as encouraging others to become fully involved, Tom and Bettie Durrant travelled all over the country, locating and identifying old camellias. In this research they were assisted by the Australian experts Professor Waterhouse and Tom Savige. In 1964 Colonel Durrant was able to import from China some Yunnan reticulata camellias not known previously in the Western world, and he was to become particularly knowledgeable about the species *C. reticulata.*

This garden, which overlooks Lake Rotorua in the central North Island of New Zealand, features an extensive selection of camellias in harmony with many other fine ornamentals.

In New Zealand there have been many worthwhile hybridising achievements. In the 1950s Dr Brian Doak, by crossing *C. saluenensis* with *C. reticulata* 'Captain Rawes', produced an interesting group of hybrids, which included the well-known 'Phyl Doak', 'Barbara Clark' and 'Brian'. Mention has already been made of the Jury brothers, Jim Finlay, Neville Haydon, Os Blumhardt, Trevor Lennard and John Lesnie (see pages 27 and 31). One of Neville Haydon's recent introductions, 'Takanini', is likely to become even more popular because of the richness of its colour and its long flowering season, which begins before many sasanquas.

Os Blumhardt has raised two very dark, black-red-flowered hybrids using pollen from *C. japonica* 'Kuro-tsubaki'. 'Night Rider' and 'Black Opal' are eye-catching blooms because of their colour. His fragrant 'Sugar Dream' is another popular plant. John Lesnie has raised the beautiful *C. japonica* 'Queen Diana', as well as the fragrant *C. lutchuensis* hybrid 'Quintessence'.

Since this great post-war revival of interest, camellias have been planted extensively in public as well as private gardens. Eden Garden in Auckland, established nearly thirty years ago under the direction of Jack Clark, has an extensive collection of camellias that were available after the Second World War. With newer varieties being added each year, Eden Garden now presents a brilliant display of large, older cultivars alongside the most recent introductions. The many hundreds of camellias are interspersed with numerous other trees and shrubs to give an ever-changing spectacle of colour and form.

The botanic gardens in the four main centres of Auckland, Wellington,

Camellias present a colourful display in Pollard Park, Blenheim, one of many extensive plantings in public gardens throughout New Zealand.

'Takanini', raised by Neville Haydon, has an exceptionally long flowering season.

'Margaret Hilford', a chance seedling from Eden Garden, raised by the author.

'Scentuous', a fragrant hybrid resulting from Jim Finlay's extensive search for this quality.

'Dream Boat', an outstanding *C.* x *williamsii* formal double hybrid, bred by Felix Jury.

Four New Zealand-raised cultivars.

Christchurch and Dunedin have large camellia collections, and it would be hard to find a New Zealand community of any size that did not have at least a small group of camellias growing in public parks and gardens or lining streets. The Waipahihi Botanic Gardens in Taupo, the Hammond Camellia Garden in Hamilton, street plantings in Whakatane, the Bason Botanical Reserve in Whanganui, Pollard Park in Blenheim, and the public gardens in Gore are but a few of the extensive plantings giving pleasure to local residents and to visitors. The extent of community interest is well illustrated by the small Putaruru district in the Waikato, which adopted the camellia as its representative flower and has made significant plantings in parks, reserves and streets.

When the camellia came to Australia and New Zealand, it was to mark the beginning of a great surge of new horticultural interest. After a temporary lull, the south Pacific region took a leading place among camellia-growing nations following the Second World War. Though the camellia is best known as an ornamental plant in Australia and New Zealand, commercial tea plantations have been established in Queensland and New South Wales and, more recently, in Motueka, New Zealand. In Australia the tropical, black tea variety *C. sinensis* var. *assamica* is grown, while in New Zealand it is the hardy *C. sinensis* var. *sinensis* that is being cultivated for green tea.

Eden Garden, created in a disused quarry on the slopes of Mount Eden, Auckland, New Zealand, introduces visitors to a memorable display of old camellia cultivars alongside newer varieties.

CHAPTER 3

Choosing a camellia

The establishment and development of a garden is a very personal exercise. The final result, if there ever is a 'final' result, will reflect individual preferences in colour, form and plant companionship. Camellias have much to offer the gardener planning a new garden or rejuvenating an old one; there are very few other genera that offer so many options or are so versatile.

In this chapter, the differences in flower form and colour, foliage and growth habit are discussed. These differences will influence decisions on whether the camellia is to be planted in the open ground or in a container. Chapters 4 and 5 give more specific information about selecting camellias for the open ground, and chapter 6, selecting camellias for containers.

Flower size

Camellia flowers may be as small as 1 cm (0.4 in.) across, as on the species *C. forrestii*, they may be as large as 20 cm (8 in.), like 'Jean Pursel', or they may be any size between these extremes. Some people are confused by the term 'miniature' when applied to camellias, assuming, reasonably, that this description implies that the plant will be miniature in size. However, 'miniature' and the other terms, 'small', 'medium', 'large' and 'very large', refer to flower size, not to the ultimate height of the plant. 'Spring Festival' is one example of a miniature-flowered camellia that will naturally grow very tall if not pruned to a manageable height.

The accepted ranges for these categories of flower size are: miniature, less than 6.5 cm (2.5 in.); small, 6.5–8 cm (2.5–3 in); medium, 8–10 cm (3–4 in.); large, 10–12.5 cm (4–5 in.); very large, over 12.5 cm (5 in.). One camellia nursery includes a further category of 'tiny' for very small blooms.

Flower forms

The common classification of camellia flower forms is based mainly upon the number and arrangement of petals.

The single form of 'Yuletide', with one row of petals and conspicuous stamens.

The semi-double 'Setsugekka', showing two rows of petals and prominent stamens.

'Annette Carol' shows a loose peony form of deep, rounded flower.

The full peony form of 'Silver Chalice', a form that never shows stamens.

'Elegans Champagne', an anemone form with an intermingled mass of petaloids and stamens.

'Harold L. Paige', which may vary from rose-form double, with imbricated petals, to peony form.

'Nuccio's Gem', always formal double but sometimes with the rows of petals in tiers.

'Demi-Tasse', a small to medium semi-double flower of hose-in-hose form.

Single: One row of not more than eight petals with conspicuous stamens; the petals may be regular, irregular or loose, e.g. 'Spencer's Pink', 'Yuletide', 'Yuri-tsubaki', 'Yukimiguruma' (known generally but incorrectly as 'Amabilis').

Semi-double: Two or more rows of regular, irregular or loose petals with conspicuous stamens, e.g. 'Nicky Crisp', 'Moonlight Bay', 'Guilio Nuccio', 'Pavlova', 'Setsugekka', 'Tiny Star'.

Peony form or informal double: A mass of raised petals with petaloids (parts of the flower that have assumed the appearance of small, narrow or twisted petals). There is a wide diversity within this group. Stamens may be in a small, central group, mostly hidden by the raised petals, or they may be interspersed among the petals. The deep, rounded flower has two forms: a loose peony form, e.g. 'Annette Carol', 'Dixie Knight'; and a full peony form, e.g. 'Debutante', 'El Dorado', 'Madame Picouline', 'Silver Chalice'.

Anemone form: One or more layers of large outer petals with a mass of petaloids and stamens in the centre, e.g. 'Elegans Champagne', 'Jury's Yellow', 'Maui'.

Rose-form double: Several layers of overlapping petals showing stamens in the centre when fully opened, e.g. 'Jubilation', 'Mary Agnes Patin', 'Spring Festival', 'Harold L. Paige'. Most varieties in this group may vary, say, from semi-double to rose-form double, or from rose-form double to formal double.

Formal double: Several layers of overlapping petals arranged symmetrically, never showing stamens, e.g. 'Desire', 'Amazing Graces', 'Alba Plena', 'Dream Boat', 'Nuccio's Gem'.

Within these basic classifications of flower form there may be other notable differences. A single flower may be flat in arrangement or it may be tubular. Some of those described as formal double may occasionally present the petals arranged in tiers. Other cultivars may have their petals organised in a distinctive 'hose-in-hose' arrangement, giving the appearance of one bloom inside another, or a cup-and-saucer effect. The simple description of, for example, 'Guilio Nuccio' as semi-double does not give any indication of that flower's distinctive 'rabbit ear' centre.

The flowers of some varieties may be ruffled, fluted, fimbriated or curved. They may be broad, round, narrow or long. In some flowers there is a clear distinction between petals and stamens, while in others, petals, stamens and petaloids intermingle.

Variations may also be found in the form of different flowers of the same cultivar. Such variations may occur regularly, or appear in different localities, or be due to temperature or to the season.

Flower colour

One of the main considerations in selecting a camellia is the colour of the blooms. Camellias range in colour from white, through shades of pink to deepest red. In recent years two yellow-flowered species—*C. euphlebia*, from Vietnam, and *C. chrysantha*—have been made available to Western horticulturists. Plants of *C. chrysantha* can now be obtained from specialist nurseries. However, even if the protection this plant needs is given, it may still be disappointing, because the small, yellow flowers may not appear for several years and then sparsely. Fortunately, the foliage is sure to give much pleasure, for it is a handsome plant.

The shades of red camellia flowers cover an extensive range, including the very dark, nearly black blooms of, for example, 'Night Rider', 'Black Lace' and 'Black Tie', the dark red 'Midnight' or 'Bob Hope', the scarlet 'Jingan-cha', and the wine-red, 'Mark Alan'. There are many other shades of red, varying in intensity of colour, with descriptions such as 'cherry-red', 'carmine', 'turkey-red' or 'deep red'.

There is wide variation, similarly, in the range of pink blooms available. Options include the light, blush-pink of, say, 'Twilight', the soft pink of 'Lovely Lady' or 'Patricia Coull', the medium, orchid-pink of 'Lois Shinault', the lavender-pinks typified by 'Pink Dahlia' or the bright pink with lavender cast of 'Dream Boat'.

Many camellias with clear, white blooms are offered for sale, e.g. 'White Nun', 'Silver Chalice' and 'Silver Cloud'.

Camellia flowers with cream to primrose-yellow centre petaloids sur-

'Night Rider' is a very dark black-red colour inherited from its parent 'Kuro-tsubaki'.

'Jury's Yellow', white with cream centre petaloids, is very similar to 'Brushfield's Yellow'.

'Jubilation', a pink flower that sometimes has the colour broken up by a deeper pink fleck.

'Scented Gem', with white petaloids contrasting with the surrounding fuchsia-pink petals.

rounded by off-white guard petals delight many gardeners. 'Brushfield's Yellow' and the very similar 'Gwenneth Morey', both from Australia, as well as the New Zealand-raised 'Jury's Yellow', are reliable plants. The more recently available 'Dahlohnega', with its cream to canary yellow, small to medium-sized, formal double flowers is likely to have many admirers.

The colour options are widened by a great number of combinations of reds, pinks and whites, and even variations of red or pink in the one flower. The combinations may take various forms, as the following examples show:

'Ballet Dancer', cream shading to coral-pink at edges
'Betty's Beauty', white with red edge
'Can Can', pale pink with darker pink veining and petal edges
'Cinnamon Cindy', white with pink tinges
'Commander Mulroy', blush-pink to white edged pink with pink bud centre
'Desire', white to pale pink with darker pink edges
'Grace Albritton', white with pink edging
'Hawaii', pink with white petal edges
'Himatsuri', marbled red and white
'Just Sue', light pink with petals bordered red
'Lady Loch', light pink with petals edged white
'Scentuous', white with pink flush on reverse of petals

'Nuccio's Pearl' has another colour combination, white shaded with orchid-pink.

'Dixie Knight Supreme', with the deep red of 'Dixie Knight' heavily broken by white.

'Wirlinga Princess', pale pink fading to white at centre with deeper pink under petals

No camellia flowers are distinctly blue in colour, although a blue or purple tint does affect the purity of colour in some of the dark reds. There are a few camellias whose names, at least, suggest a tendency towards blue: 'Blue Bird' is described as deep pink with a blue cast; 'Blue Blood' as rose-pink with blue overtones; and 'Blue Danube' as rose-lavender. The Portuguese cultivar 'Donna Herzilia de Freitas Magalhaes' is described as 'red with distinct violet shade'.

Variegated flowers with irregular white blotches on red or pink petals are often found. Some variegations in colour are regular in their pattern, indicating that the variegation is genetic, occurring naturally in the plant; others appear as irregular blotches and have been introduced by grafting, usually deliberately but sometimes inadvertently, onto virus-infected stock.

Variegated forms have been bred for many varieties. These blotched blooms are identified by the word 'variegated' after the cultivar name—for example 'Guilio Nuccio Variegated'. 'Ville de Nantes' is an exception; this is the name of the variegated form of the solid-coloured 'Ville de Nantes Red'. It is worth noting here that genetic variegation will have no effect on the vigour of a plant, whereas virus-induced variegation will weaken its health.

The intensity of colour in the same variety may vary from one garden to another. The pH level, the fertilisers used, the trace elements in the soil, and the climatic conditions may, separately and together, influence the depth of colour. An acidic soil tends to increase the brightness of colour, while iron in the soil or fertiliser makes the colour of a camellia flower more vivid and the foliage a richer green. If the general health of camellias is maintained through effective cultural practices, there should be little concern about the quality of colour displayed. The effect of climatic conditions is indicated by the fact that camellias grown in greenhouses usually lack the purity of colour found in those grown outdoors.

Flowering season

The flowering season of different varieties and species offers further choice. By selecting plants carefully, camellias can be flowering in the garden in early autumn, sometimes starting even in late summer. Other varieties will give pleasure with their colourful displays through winter, while some will continue on into the spring. Suggestions for early, mid-season and late-flowering varieties are given in chapter 5, page 97. An extended list of camellia species and cultivars, suitable for all situations, on page 156, provides a brief description of each variety and gives an indication of the flowering time.

Foliage

The striking variety of foliage adds as much to the charm of camellias as the flowers. Each species has characteristic foliage. Though the leaves of different *C. japonica* cultivars may vary in size and shape, they are noted for their smoothness and glossy, green colour. *C. reticulata* produces leaves that are a duller, dark green colour and much larger. *C. chrysantha* and *C. granthamiana* have large leaves, leathery in texture and deep veined, the former a shiny green and the latter a dull green.

The new growth on some species and cultivars captivates many admirers. The reddish bronze of the *C.* x *williamsii* hybrid 'Elegant Beauty' and the bronze of *C. saluenensis* or *C. chrysantha* are fine examples of attractively coloured new growth. Perhaps the finest of all is the bronze-coloured *C. salicifolia*. Other spectacular foliage includes the dark red, new leaves of 'Black Opal' and 'Night Rider'.

The size of the leaves in relation to the size of the flowers is important in the overall attractiveness of a camellia. The leaves of different species vary considerably in size and proportions, for example *C. lutchuensis* has leaves about 3 x 1.5 cm (1 x 0.5 in.), *C. japonica*, 8.5 x 4 cm (3 x 1.5 in.), and *C. reticulata*, 11 x 5 cm (4 x 2 in.). Most camellia leaves are elliptic, widest at or about the middle and narrowing equally to the ends, but variations show in, for example, *C. forrestii*, with leaves pointed at both ends, *C. transnokoensis*, tapering to a blunt apex, or *C. reticulata*, with prominent leaf veins. The

The large, quilted leaves of *C. chrysantha*, showing its bronze-coloured new growth.

'Black Opal' produces thick new foliage, a dark bronze or red colour.

'Kingyo-tsubaki', the goldfish camellia, named for its distinctive fishtail leaves.

'Reigyoku' is grown for its choice green and gold foliage, coloured pink when young.

'Hakuhan-kujaku', the peacock camellia, with distinctly curled leaves, and flowers at the stem tips

leaves of *C. tsaii* are long and narrow, 6 x 2 cm (2 x 0.75 in.).

Camellia species have flowers appropriate to their leaf size, but hybrids bred from them do not always inherit their parents' characteristics. Those with, for example, small flowers and large leaves are rarely admired and soon disappear from the gardening scene. *C. reticulata* and its hybrids such as 'Dr Clifford Parks' or 'Debut', with large flowers in proportion to large leaves, are pleasing in their effect. So too are the small-leafed varieties with small flowers, such as 'Alpen Glo', 'Scented Gem', 'Spring Festival' and 'Isaribi'.

Some cultivars exhibit special distinguishing features. 'Kingyo-tsubaki', the 'goldfish camellia', is well known for its divided or fishtail leaves. 'Hakuhan-kujaku', the peacock camellia, presents a long, narrow leaf that curls distinctly. There are also differences in the degree of serration of leaf edges, with some, like 'Elegans Champagne', having prominent serrations.

The uniform patterns of variegation that occur naturally in the leaves of some camellias can provide interesting variation in the garden. Prominent among these are the 'Bentens', notable for their brilliantly coloured green leaves, uniformly edged with creamy yellow, white or a paler green. This pattern of leaf colour, which is of genetic origin, can be expected on camellias that include 'Benten' in their name—for example, 'Benten-kagura', 'Benten-tsubaki' or 'Tafuku-benten'. Without doubt, though, the most striking of this group of choice-foliage varieties is 'Reigyoku'. Its green and gold leaves, with the gold sections a bright pink when young, stand out in the garden.

Growth habits

Selection and placement of camellias in the garden may be influenced by the growth habits of different varieties. Some plants are narrow and columnar, some weeping, with long pendulous branches, while others are compact and bushy. There are those that are unlikely ever to be more than a metre tall and those that, if unrestricted, will grow into very tall trees.

Descriptions of growth habit will usually include a reference to the rate of growth, indicated by the terms 'slow', 'medium', 'vigorous' or 'fast'. In most descriptions of camellias one of these expressions is combined with an explanation of the nature of that growth. 'Dwarf, compact growth' in reference to 'Baby Bear' indicates a very small, tightly branched plant. 'Baby Willow', described as having 'dwarf, weeping growth', though still extremely small and slow growing, sends out loosely hanging branches. 'Slow, upright growth' shows that 'Nicky Crisp', for example, will grow upwards rather than spread out, but will take longer than those described as having 'medium, upright growth' to reach the same height. Any variety said to be of 'vigorous, upright growth' will become a tall plant very quickly. 'Spreading', 'pendulous' and 'weeping' are terms used to indicate that the plant will send out long lateral branches that in some cases will arch over or 'weep'. Other expressions, such as 'open', 'bushy' or 'dense', are self-explanatory.

The space available for the plant should also be considered. While it is possible to control size through regular, judicious pruning, it is preferable to select a variety with a growth habit that will make it fit attractively in the

Different camellias have different growth habits. 'Bellbird' has strong, bushy but spreading growth.

GROWTH HABITS

Slow growing:
'Baby Bear'
'Itty Bit'
'Nicky Crisp'
'Snippet'

Fast growing:
'Alpen Glo'
'Burgundy Boy'
'Fairy Wand'
'Japanese Fantasy'

Slender:
'Cinnamon Cindy'
'Memento'
'Red Red Rose'
'Spring Festival'

Weeping:
'Dave's Weeper'
'Rosiflora Cascade'
'Wirlinga Belle'
'Wirlinga Gem'

Bushy:
'Alba Plena'
'Ballet Queen'
'Nicky Crisp'
'Pink Cameo'

Upright:
'Bokuhan' ('Tinsie')
'Cornelian'
'Lois Shinault'
'Nymph'

Tall:
'China Doll'
'Kumagai' (Nagoya)
'Mary Phoebe Taylor'
'Virginia Franco Rosea'

Dwarf:
'Baby Bear'
'Baby Willow'
'The Elf'
'Sasanqua Compacta'

'Bokuhan'

New seedling 'Rambling Rose'

Opposite: The beautiful formal double *C. japonica* 'Desire' is a vigorous plant with upright, compact growth appropriate for many situations. In partial shade, 'Desire' will reward the grower with many beautiful blooms.

'Purple Gown', with the dark green leaves indicative of a healthy plant, makes a colourful display.

space. Varieties like 'Spring Festival' and 'Cinnamon Cindy' or species like *C. transnokoensis*, with their tall, columnar growth, are ideal in small areas. Others, like 'Baby Bear', 'Nicky Crisp' or 'Quintessence', have the slow growth that makes them desirable low-growing plants. The description of varieties included in the annotated list of camellia species and cultivars, page 156, offers a more exact definition of each cultivar's growth habits.

The wide range of species and cultivars with varying size, form, colour or growth habit means that there are camellias for any situation. With so many options available, it may be difficult to make a final selection, but with a little patience and observation, a camellia eminently suitable for the use and the location can be obtained.

Perhaps the best advice for selecting a camellia is to discuss the possibilities with other growers in the district. They can advise on the best varieties for the area and any difficulties there might be. It is always worth noting very carefully how different varieties perform in similar situations to yours. Walking around neighbouring streets and visiting gardens, including botanic gardens and other public plantings, can help in identifying varieties that thrive locally. Camellias that are spectacular in some districts may be less successful elsewhere. Some that produce a few blooms of exquisite beauty may also produce a large number of inconsistent size and form.

Buying a camellia

The first rule is to buy from a reputable grower or garden centre. A supplier who is a member of a camellia society will have access to the most up-to-date information and can give the best advice. Look around, too, because the price as well as the quality of the plants may vary considerably. A higher price does not guarantee a better quality plant.

Nurseries specialising in propagating camellias are likely to offer the healthiest plants at the most competitive prices, and also offer the best advice. With their horticultural life revolving so much around camellias, these nurseries have a deep knowledge of the genus. Those who maintain close contacts with growers and hybridists in other countries are able to present the most extensive ranges of new and old varieties.

When selecting a plant, look closely at the foliage—the leaves will proclaim the plant's health. Plants that seem undernourished, with yellowish leaves, or show stress by wilting or by leaves that have brown patches on the edges, should be avoided. Disorders are discussed in some detail in chapter 7.

The most important thing for a new plant is to have a strong root system. This is far more important than size. Of course, the root system cannot be seen, so these other indicators of the health of the plant must be noted.

Most plants are sold in plastic planter bags. Strong root growth appearing from the drainage holes underneath probably indicates that the plant is rootbound—the roots have outgrown the space available and become a tangled mass. If this condition is accompanied by foliage that is under stress, do not take the plant. If the plant looks otherwise healthy, it is possible to loosen the roots by gently hosing off the soil before planting. It is often preferable to select a small plant rather than a larger one in the same-sized planter bag. The smaller one probably has a better root-to-leaf ratio than the larger one and will soon grow to a good size. Be particularly wary of camellias offered in reduced-price sales. They are likely to have been held for a considerable time without having been repotted and will probably be rootbound.

Though it is unlikely with the bark mixes generally used today, there is always the possibility of a fungus causing root rot (see page 132) being introduced to the garden in container-grown plants from a nursery. As soon as possible, ensure that they have clean, white, healthy-looking roots. If a newly bought plant is found to suffer from root rot or any other disease, it should be returned to the nursery immediately.

CHAPTER 4

Growing camellias in the open ground

In a temperate climate, most camellias can be grown successfully in the open ground. However, the ability of camellias to withstand extremes of heat or cold is a crucial issue for growers in many geographical regions. In less favourable conditions, the basic principles for care must be adapted and, in some cases, special facilities provided, but with knowledge of local conditions and careful selection of suitable species or cultivars, it is possible to provide an environment in which plants will flourish. Plant breeders continue to search for new, hardy varieties. *C. oleifera* and the less well-known *C. shensiensis*, the most northerly growing camellia in China, may in the future be very important in this search. Any success benefits all growers, particularly those in marginal areas, and means that locations suitable for growing camellias, either with or without special protection, can be extended.

The problems of cold hardiness are of great concern to growers in the British Isles and Europe. Though many gardeners in places such as the Channel Islands and western Cornwall do not need to worry unduly about the weather, it is different further to the north of Britain and away from the coast. Varieties must be selected carefully, with *C.* x *williamsii* and other hybrids being the most suitable.

The ability of camellias to withstand heat is as much an issue in some parts of the world as their ability to tolerate cold. It says much for the vitality of the genus, and for the enthusiasm and application of growers, that camellias grow so well in Australia's varied and often extreme conditions. Australia is a vast country experiencing very hot summers, different rainfall patterns from state to state, and changing soil types, making it unsuitable for camellias in some parts and marginal in others. Carefully selected and nurtured, however, they can be exciting plants in the extreme heat of parts of Queensland and Western Australia, as well as in the sometimes sub-zero temperatures of Tas-

A well cared-for specimen of 'Terrell Weaver' is always a spectacular sight in bloom.

'Valentine Day' thrives in the open ground in the favourable New Zealand climate.

mania, or in the more temperate climates of New South Wales, Victoria and South Australia. In Victoria, camellias have survived rare snowstorms as well as heat, and severe damage is caused when winds blow from the central desert.

New Zealand has an ideal climate—in fact, some people believe that conditions here are more favourable than in the camellia homelands! As one American observer wrote in *The Camellia Journal* (August 1989), 'a camellia hobbyist in New Zealand can dig a hole, put in a camellia and watch it grow. He needs no shade cover, no watering and very little other care. This holds true for nearly every species of camellia grown in New Zealand.' Perhaps the best supporting evidence for this observation is seen in the many specimens of *C. japonica* more than 100 years old that still bloom magnificently, in spite of years of neglect.

Though there are differences in climatic conditions from the frost-free north to the colder area about 1600 kilometres (1000 miles) to the south,

Following page: Camellias with a range of colours and growth habits add wide variation to a garden in South Auckland, New Zealand, as they complement the many other trees and shrubs.

These two delicately coloured cultivars show the benefit of being grown in some shade, which protects the pink colour shading to white of 'Guest Star' and the pure white of 'Fimbriata'.

and between coastal and inland districts, generally everywhere is suitable for camellias. Most plants are grown outside in the open ground, though in some places, such as the southernmost and colder districts, some species and varieties may not thrive—for example *C. chrysantha* and *C. hongkongensis*, which produce new growth at times when frosts are likely to damage them.

New Zealanders usually think of hardiness in terms of the ability of flowers, rather than plants, to withstand weather damage. White and pale pink flowers are not as weather-resistant as the various shades of red. However, it has been found that the flowers of some *C. pitardii* hybrids can withstand low temperatures with little if any effect.

It is useful for growers to have an understanding of conditions in the camellia homelands so that efforts can be made to provide an environment as close as possible to the plant's natural habitat. In the homeland camellias grow in woodland, where a deep, acidic litter of foliage forms around them, and some shade, with high humidity, is provided. There is copious rainfall, with a soil structure that permits efficient drainage, and protection from extremes of temperature in the natural thickets and forests.

Shelter and shade

Although it is possible to grow virtually all varieties in the open, even in the most favourable environments, camellias, particularly the whites and pale pinks, will benefit from some protection from strong winds.

Cultivars of the autumn-flowering *C. sasanqua*, *C. hiemalis* and *C. vernalis* species—for example, 'Showa-no-sakae', 'Sparkling Burgundy' and 'Bert Jones'—and the later-flowering reticulata and reticulata hybrids are all very happy in full sunlight. In fact, some with red blooms, such as 'Margaret Hilford' or 'William Hertrich', are seen at their best in direct sunlight, glowing with vibrant colour. Filtered sunlight will improve the quality of white and pale pink blooms, with beautiful varieties like 'Queen Diana' and 'Desire' growing to perfection only with some shelter.

Camellias planted in full sun are liable to suffer if the soil dries out too quickly, and it is important to give some protection through careful watering and mulching, at least for the first two years until plants are well established. Observation of camellias growing locally will give an indication of whether, for example, some of the small-leafed species or hybrids prefer shading from the morning sun, or whether some *C. japonica* cultivars are especially at risk in strong sunshine. The effects of stress through adverse conditions are discussed in chapter 7.

Camellias, with an underplanting of cyclamen, bloom freely in partial shade and filtered sunlight.

Soil conditions

Camellias are reasonably tolerant of a wide range of soil environments but respond vigorously to ideal conditions—slightly acid, free-draining soil that is rich in humus.

Soil acidity or pH is measured on a scale of 1 to 14, with 7 indicating a neutral state. Higher numbers represent an increasing alkalinity, and corresponding increase in calcium, whereas numbers below 7 register a higher acidity. The pH level affects the fertility of the soil and the availability of some nutrients. Camellias are often described as acid-loving plants, but in fact it would be more accurate to describe them as being acid-tolerant, preferring soil measuring pH 6– 6.5. Although calcium is an essential mineral, camellias will not tolerate very much of it. The pH range varies considerably from garden to garden, and thousands of gardeners are growing beautiful camellias in soil that has never been tested. However, it may be useful to have the soil tested, particularly when taking over a new garden. This can be done commercially and accurately by soil experts or, with varying degrees of accuracy, by using a 'do-it-yourself' testing kit that can be obtained from a garden centre or nursery.

In a well-drained, slightly acidic soil containing plenty of organic matter, 'Mudancha' responds with a brilliant display of flowers.

The right soil conditions ensure that the vigorous, semi-double 'Guilio Nuccio' in full bloom is a spectacular sight.

Establishing a soil with a degree of acidity that is close to ideal should not be a problem. Organic material increases in acidity as it decomposes. Gardeners who follow advice to use plenty of compost will have few worries about acidity. In fact, it is recommended that a handful of dolomite lime should be added to the compost heap with each new layer of green material to counteract excessive acidity. If, when establishing a garden, it is known that the soil is very alkaline, it may be advisable to establish raised beds by adding acidic soil to a depth of about 40–50 cm (15–20 in.).

The soil in which camellias are grown should always retain some moisture but must be free-draining. Camellias object very strongly to their roots being waterlogged, that is, to having 'wet feet'. In these conditions the air is pushed out of the soil by the water, which can result in the development of a fungus causing root rot, leading to the death of the plant. In waterlogged soils, pumice or sand should be added to improve the flow of surplus water away from the roots.

Heavy clay soils can also be improved by the addition of humus or organic matter in the form of compost, which is excellent for opening up the soil as well as retaining moisture and providing nutrients. Peat is also a useful source of organic material, although it does not provide nutrients. In areas with heavy clay or waterlogged soil it is desirable to build the soil up by means of raised beds. A height of 25 cm (10 in.) above the surrounding area will make a significant difference.

In extremely heavy soil, if raising the beds and improving the soil texture are insufficient, a drainage system may have to be considered. Gardeners have sometimes been advised to dig a deep planting hole and fill the bottom with stones. This should be avoided with camellias, as all it does is provide a sump to hold the water unless some provision is made to drain it away.

The topsoil contains the humus and the organisms necessary for healthy plant growth. The deeper this layer, the better. It is here that the plants first find the essential nutrients, which are in solution and move downwards with soil water. Nutrients are lost through the leaching action of water and through absorption by plants and must be replenished regularly (see Fertilisers, page 83). The greater the quantity of humus or organic matter in the soil, the more likely it is to have all the nutrients necessary.

A very light, sandy soil, though easy to work, has difficulty retaining moisture and may lack nutrients. As with clay soil, the principal treatment is

Well cared-for camellias add charm and elegance to the patio of a home in Melbourne, Australia.

This handsome specimen of 'Pharaoh' is thriving in deeply dug, well-drained soil.

to add organic matter, both when preparing the soil for planting and as mulch.

Poorly prepared subsoil may contribute to drainage problems and will also lack adequate nutrients and micro-organisms. When preparing the planting site, every effort should be made to break up and loosen the subsoil without bringing it to the surface. If the subsoil already drains readily, be thankful.

There is another reason for breaking up the subsoil as much as possible. One of the myths often perpetuated about camellias is that they are shallow-rooted. In fact, they send down roots deep into the soil if they can, and naturally have strong, deeply penetrating tap-roots. Plants purchased from nurseries and garden centres are either grown from cuttings or grafted onto seedlings that have had the original tap-root pinched off. Their root systems will vary in development but will benefit by being able to range deeply and widely through suitable soil.

Planting

Dig a wide hole, as much as four times as wide as the container and at least twice as deep. Put back into the bottom of the hole a mixture of soil and compost, about two-thirds soil to one-third compost, depending on the quality of the soil, leaving enough room for the plant. The vital thing is to have a mixture that is rich in well-rotted organic matter. It may be preferable to obtain one of the commercially prepared soil mixes, which have a loose texture with a high humus content and incorporate fertilisers.

If not using a fertiliser-enriched, commercial soil mix, fertiliser should be added to the soil in the bottom of the hole. This is the only time that it will be possible to place nutrients directly under the plant, so it is worth taking advantage of the opportunity. A handful of a slow-release fertiliser will provide nutrients for some months, or a mixture prepared specifically for 'acid-loving' plants or a general fertiliser suitable for shrubs could be used. Another possibility is to add a good handful of superphosphate mixed with blood and bone and a little dolomite lime. Remember, however, when using inorganic fertilisers other than the slow-release pellets, to be sure that they are mixed thoroughly with the soil and do not come in direct contact with the roots.

Firm the soil in the bottom of the hole. The level must be such that the top of the soil around the roots of the plant will be slightly above the surrounding ground level when the plant is in position. When the plant finally settles, it will be the same depth in the garden as it was in its planter bag.

While the plant is still in its container, water it thoroughly and allow the surplus to drain away. This can be done by immersing the plant in a bucket of water to cover the planter bag, and leaving it until air bubbles stop coming to the surface.

Slit the sides of the plastic planter bag and remove it carefully, avoiding damaging the roots. The bottom roots should be loosened and spread out. If they are too tightly intertwined and wound round the inside of the bag, hose them very gently to loosen them. This will allow them to spread out easily. Place the plant in position in the hole and fill around it with the compost/soil mix, firm it down carefully and water thoroughly.

If the camellia is to be supported, a stake should be driven into the ground before planting to avoid damaging the roots. Some tree experts claim that anchoring a young tree too firmly can hinder the development of a strong root system. If you do provide this support, use as short a stake as possible and remove it as soon as the plant is secure in the ground.

Mulching

Camellias in the wild benefit from a ground cover of leaves and branches forming a deep litter. As the litter breaks down, soil fertility and texture are improved and nutrients are provided. The litter also conserves moisture,

Opposite: 'San Marino' shows the benefits of a straw mulch, which conserves moisture and protects the roots while supplying nutrients as it breaks down.

A mulch gives the roots of camellias the protection they need. Left: 'Limelight', with low-growing plants. Right: 'Kiwi Triumph' benefits from a natural litter.

while protecting the roots from extremes of soil temperature.

Gardeners can recreate this forest litter by using a mulch consisting of organic materials such as leaves, thinly spread grass clippings, bark, chopped-up twigs and small branches, partially decomposed compost, untreated sawdust and wood shavings, straw and hay, peat moss and pine needles. Mulch should be applied at least out to the dripline of each camellia to a depth of 5–7 cm (2–3 in.), but it should not touch the plant's trunk. If the ground is dry, the soil must be watered thoroughly before applying the mulch. If peat is being used as a mulch, it is wise to soak it in a tub of water before spreading it on the ground. It should also be incorporated into the existing topsoil to prevent it drying out and blowing away. Don't forget that tea leaves are processed camellia leaves. Save them up and spread them around the camellias. They can do nothing but good.

Organic material needs a good supply of nitrogen to assist decomposition. If nothing is added, this nitrogen will be obtained from the soil to the detriment of the plant. Spreading a small quantity of blood and bone on the ground underneath the mulch will avoid this problem. This is especially important if sawdust is used.

Other materials can be used to protect the roots, to keep the soil moist, to keep the soil temperature uniform, and to suppress weeds, but they will do nothing to increase the humus content of the soil. Stones packed around are excellent for conserving moisture and keeping the roots cool. Newspaper laid out about six sheets thick, with the edges buried to prevent them blowing about, will do the work but will not add anything to the beauty of the garden. Black plastic sheeting may also be used but it can cause very high soil temperatures and, ultimately, it will break down and become a nuisance around the garden. Weedmat can be obtained from garden centres and has the advantage of preventing the growth of weeds while allowing water to pass through it and also conserving soil moisture.

Mulching is a vital step in the care of camellias, particularly young plants. The mulch should be maintained throughout the year, but it is most beneficial during the summer and winter months.

Fertilisers

Plants require a balanced diet of the major nutrient elements, nitrogen (N), phosphorous (P), potassium (K), calcium (Ca), magnesium (Mg), sulphur (S), and a range of trace elements, including iron (Fe), manganese (Mn), copper (Cu) and zinc (Zn), which are needed in very small amounts. Nitrogen promotes growth, potassium encourages the development of healthy leaves and

The rich colour of these 'Valentine Day' blooms is the reward for ensuring that all the necessary nutrients are provided.

flowers, and phosphorous develops healthy roots and flowers, and with potassium and magnesium increases the strength and hardiness of the plant.

If a camellia is unable to obtain sufficient of any one of the nutrients it needs, its growth and appearance will be affected adversely. Signs of nutritional deficiencies likely to be noticed first are a yellowing of the leaves and poor-quality flowers. These are discussed in more detail on page 129.

Camellias give a good indication of their general health when developing the vegetative or growth buds before spring, and again in autumn for japonicas and some hybrids. If the plant is in good general health, these buds will fatten and develop strongly. If they do not increase in size, ready to burst into new leaf, there is certainly a problem and all cultural practices should be checked. Some gardeners, not noticing the condition of these leaf-buds, assume that a heavy flower-bud set shows that the plant is in good health. This is not a satisfactory indicator. While it is true that some varieties regularly develop clusters of buds, it is also true that a plant in poor health may set many flower-buds in an effort to form seed and keep the line going before it dies. The condition of the leaf-buds gives a more accurate picture of the plant's health.

If a slow-release fertiliser is used at the time of planting, there should be no need for any additional feeding for some time. If a mulch of organic matter or compost is maintained around camellias (see page 80), there will be little other feeding required. Together, the fertiliser and the compost will supply most, if not all, of the nutrients needed until the plant is well established.

Animal manures are best incorporated in compost and allowed to break down with the other organic materials. Poultry manure, because it is very strong, with an extremely high nitrogen content, should only be used in this way. Processed sheep pellets or dry, aged animal manure spread around a camellia can be useful tonics, as they contain basic nutrients as well as a wide range of trace elements.

Many people today are committed to 'organic' gardening and insist on using organic fertilisers only. Plants do not discriminate and will absorb nutrients in solution regardless of whether they were applied in organic or inorganic form. Inorganic fertilisers may be added on their own or in combination with compost and animal manures. Commercial fertilisers have a code indicating the composition of the mixture. The code N5.P5.K5 shows that the nitrogen, phosphorous and potassium are in equal proportions. Fertiliser for 'acid-loving' camellias, rhododendrons and azaleas is usually N10.P5.K5. If trace elements are included in the mix, this also will be noted.

When using these mixtures remember to apply them sparingly. It is often claimed that more camellias are killed by overfeeding than from neglect. Approximately 80–100 grams (roughly a small handful) per square metre

Opposite: Plants that enjoy free-draining, slightly acid soil rich in humus should be chosen to complement camellias. Here, magnolias are outstanding companions.

(2–3 oz per square yard) is ample. As the tree grows, the quantity can be increased in the same proportion and applied to cover the area from about 15 cm (6 in.) away from the trunk to beyond the dripline. The ground must be well watered before fertilisers are applied, and they should be watered in after application. It is important to ensure that the fertiliser goes on to the soil, not the foliage; any on the foliage should be washed off immediately. If it stays on the foliage for long, severe burning will result. The loss of nutrients through leaching will be quicker when chemical or inorganic fertilisers are used. By spreading organic matter around the plants, nutrients will be released steadily into the soil over a long period.

Although camellias are often described as 'lime-haters', they must have some calcium. This can be provided by applying dolomite lime, which has the other advantages of making magnesium available and, when a large amount of compost has been spread around, counteracting too much acidity.

Organic matter or fertilisers spread on the ground will ultimately be absorbed in solution through the roots. There is a place also for foliar feeding or spraying plant food onto the leaves. There are several commercial preparations available from garden centres, including a fish fertiliser and liquid blood and bone incorporating trace elements. A weak solution can be applied about once a month, preferably in the early morning or evening.

Whatever type of fertiliser is used, a little feeding regularly will be far more beneficial than a massive application once or twice a year. Larger applications are best given towards the end of winter so that the nutrients are available to the plant as it breaks into the new season's growth. Some growers give their main topdressing in early spring or late winter with another application in the autumn. A fertiliser with a high nitrogen content should be avoided in the autumn, as there is a danger that unseasonal new growth that may result will be damaged by bad weather. Potassic superphosphate (30%) is satisfactory as an autumn fertiliser but should be used at about half the rate suggested earlier.

Watering

The importance of a free-draining but moisture-retentive soil and the use of mulch has been emphasised. An adequate supply of water is also one of the most critical factors in successfully growing camellias—problems with camellias are often said to be due to too much water or not enough. Too little water over the summer months and a young plant will wilt, drop its leaves and die. After a couple of seasons, a healthy camellia is more able to withstand a period of drought. The failure of mature plants to form flower-buds or a tendency to drop buds in winter could be due to insufficient water in the summer.

If there is no moisture in the root zone, a build-up in the concentration of salts, which could cause burning, may affect both roots and foliage.

It is important to provide water when it is needed, avoiding any possibility of the roots drying out. Even with a mulch, care must be taken to ensure that the soil underneath is moist. A small sprinkling of water is of little use; a good soaking once a week, taking the water right down to the deepest root zone, is necessary. Camellias enjoy having their foliage sprinkled, which is best done in the evenings.

Various sprinkling systems are available. These can be very useful, but care must be taken to ensure that the water is reaching well down into the soil, while also ensuring that it is not being wasted. In extremely dry climates, trickle irrigation can be effective. With young plants it is possible to set a pipe down into the soil enabling water to reach well down into the root zone. This can be very useful in times of water shortage. A field tile or short length (20–25 cm/8–10 in.) of large-diameter plastic pipe, sunk into the ground close to the plant, will allow water to be taken to the roots without any loss from evaporation.

Pruning

Pruning is one of the most important activities in the care of camellias. Gardeners who do not prune their camellias will have, after a few years, a mass of foliage where there should be an attractive specimen. Pruning will result in healthier, better-shaped camellias that can be kept to a manageable size. Not only will the foliage benefit, but blooms will be less prone to damage from wind and rain, as they will be able to move without rubbing against closely growing leaves and branches or other blooms.

The aim of pruning is to have a plant that is open to air and light. This can be done by removing dead wood, weak and spindly growth, and straggling branches that cross awkwardly over others. The often-repeated remark that 'a bird should be able to fly through a camellia' provides a useful guideline (depending upon the size of the bird!). Few, if any, flowers will develop in the centre darkness of a plant that is untouched; and if flowers do develop there, they will not be seen anyway. Thrips, scale and other undesirables are likely to flourish in the centre, so light and air moving through an open plant will discourage them and improve the plant's general health.

An important benefit of pruning is that the plant's energy is being used to produce branches and foliage that are wanted, not wasted in growth that will be removed.

The shaping and opening up of a camellia can start as soon as it is planted. A choice can be made between pruning to establish a small tree with a single main trunk or allowing two or three strong branches to develop in the form of a shrub. Whatever is decided, growth close to the ground should be removed, as this will rarely be attractive, and any blooms here are likely to be spoilt by dirt and splashes. By keeping the lowest branches off the ground, a clear area will be available for planting some of the many ground

Light filtering through 'Debbie' after pruning ensures that pests are not likely to be attracted to the centre of the plant.

covers that are excellent companions for camellias (see page 112).

As the tree grows, its shape can be maintained by rubbing or twisting off unwanted leaf-buds before they open in spring and develop into new branches. Remove those that appear likely to grow awkwardly or to cause overcrowding. This will lead to a more open plant and will eliminate the need for some of the later, heavy pruning.

Light pruning can be done at any time of the year and will make the main pruning task much easier. Keep the secateurs clean, sharp and handy, and remove delinquent branches whenever you notice them. Picking blooms can also be part of the pruning process. Look carefully at the stem or branch before cutting, then take it back to a point that will enhance the tree's shape and openness. When shortening branches, cut back to a leaf-bud pointed in a desirable direction.

The main annual pruning should be carried out before the new spring growth has started or is too far advanced—as soon as each camellia finishes flowering. This may necessitate losing a few late blooms. If pruning is delayed for too long, it is possible that there will be few, if any, blooms the following year.

In the past it was usual to remove branches flush with the trunk. Today, however, tree researchers suggest that this is damaging to the tree and advocate cutting on an angle from the top of the branch, outside the ridge of bark where the branch joins the trunk, to a point outside the branch collar (see diagram). The branch rings and collar in this section will prevent the entry of disease, providing they are not damaged. When a branch is removed using a saw, particularly a chainsaw, there will be some rough edges that will be slow to callus. These may be smoothed off using a very sharp knife, but great care must be taken not to cut so deeply that the branch rings and collar are damaged. It would be better not to smooth the cuts with a sharp knife on a small camellia if there is any risk of cutting through the plant's protective screen.

When faced with pruning a camellia that has been neglected for several years and has become a mass of tangled branches, dead wood and thick foliage, most people wonder where to start. The best approach is to force your

Left: This camellia has been pruned to encourage a single trunk. Centre: Several leaders give the plant a bushy appearance. Right: 'Hatrack' pruning can rejuvenate old or neglected camellias.

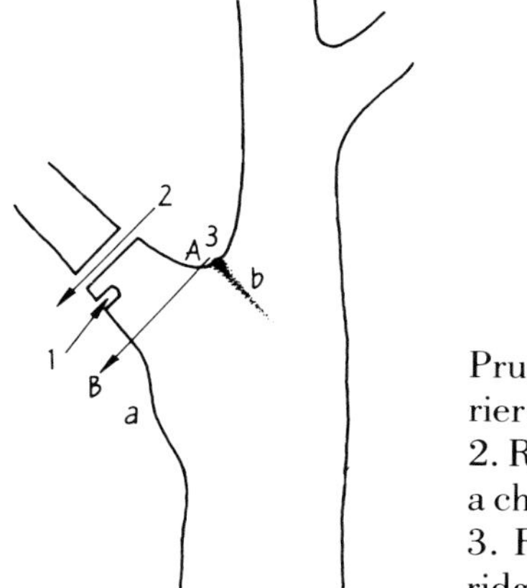

Pruning to leave a natural protective barrier: 1. Make the first small cut here. 2. Remove the branch at this point (if using a chainsaw, cut in the opposite direction). 3. Remove the stub at A–B outside the ridge of bark (b) and branch collar (a).

way into the centre and, with lopping shears or a pruning saw, cut off a large branch to create some working space. When this has been done it will be possible to see the pattern of pruning that could be followed. With some space to work in, dead wood, spindly and crossing-over branches can be reached and taken out. From then on, pruning is simply a matter of opening up the centre and shaping the camellia to a pleasing form.

Decisions about width and height must be made too. Camellias kept to a height of 1.5–2 metres (5–6.5 feet) are probably most suitable for the home garden, as they can be cared for from top to bottom, and the highest blooms can be easily seen and reached. In a large garden, however, there is a place for a camellia, particularly a reticulata, to be allowed to grow to its full grandeur.

Drastic pruning of an old camellia can be an excellent tonic for it. The term 'hatrack' pruning became popular when Colonel Tom Durrant showed that, contrary to popular belief, mature camellias, including reticulatas, could be heavily pruned—in fact reduced to a bare frame or 'hatrack'. Any camellia species that has outgrown its space or has an ill-nourished appearance can be subjected to this treatment. A chainsaw may be necessary to remove the very large branches found on an old tree. If this seemingly drastic treatment is carried out before the spring growth, new leaf-buds will soon appear.

Modern research indicates that pruning paste is not necessary, but some experienced camellia growers believe that painting the open ends of large cuts with wood preservative paint is desirable. However, the best way to ensure quick callusing of the wound and to prevent disease is to remove the branch correctly.

Disbudding

Many gardeners are horrified at the suggestion that they should remove flower-buds. There are, however, good reasons for disbudding. Some camellia varieties set clusters of buds that, if not touched, will produce small, misshapen flowers. Flower-buds can be removed by holding the branch or stem firmly with one hand and twisting the unwanted buds off with the other, leaving no more than two buds at each cluster. Buds that are obviously facing the wrong way should also be removed. Be careful not to remove a leaf-bud by mistake. By taking care to leave an assortment of large and small buds, a longer flowering season can be ensured. If you are uncertain whether to remove a bud that is facing downwards or one that is facing up, bear in mind that the one facing downwards will evolve into a flower that gives itself some protection and is therefore better for picking, while the other one will make for a brighter garden display.

Growers keen to exhibit blooms, and not so concerned about the garden display of a quantity of blooms, could remove most of the buds on each stem, leaving only one at the tip. This should give bigger and better blooms.

'Contemplation' is a splendid sight in full bloom. Disbudding of a camellia of this type is not necessary.

This cluster of buds, if left untouched, will result in an unattractive group of cramped and malformed flowers.

Most of the buds have been removed, leaving one to develop fully with adequate space for a well-formed bloom.

Thorough care, including disbudding when necessary, will produce exhibition-quality blooms. The solitary blooms of 'Kathryn Funari' (left) and 'Royal Velvet' have been allowed space to develop to perfection.

It must be emphasised that, like so many other gardening activities, disbudding is a matter of choice. Some varieties are more suited to disbudding than others; it would be wrong to suggest that this should be a common practice with all camellias. The newer, small-flowered hybrids would lose much of their garden charm with a reduced display. It would not be desirable to disbud a camellia like 'Donation' or any other variety grown for its spectacular cover of blooms.

Do not rush into disbudding as soon as the flower-buds can be identified. Some camellias will have a natural tendency to drop buds, and early disbudding may result in very few flowers at all.

Transplanting camellias

Any camellia, large or small, can be moved to a new position. Unlike many other plants, the camellia is dormant when it is flowering. Camellias should be transplanted at this time, from late autumn through winter to early spring, when the atmosphere is cooler and damper. In warmer climates where spring growth starts earlier, transplanting should be completed in winter, well before the new growth starts. A plant must be given as long as possible to become established in its new position before facing the heat of the following summer.

Before transplanting, it is desirable to prune the mass of foliage to reduce the loss of water by transpiration from the leaves. How heavily this is done will depend upon the size of the tree and the extent to which the root system will be reduced in size for shifting. If the camellia has been in position for one or two seasons only, it should be possible to lift it with the root system intact. In this case a light pruning and the removal of all flowers and flower-buds will be sufficient.

It is more difficult to transplant a camellia that has become well established with a very strong root system. Heavy pruning to remove most of the foliage will be necessary. If possible, the plant should be wrenched in early spring, well before the planned move, by pushing a sharp spade deep into the soil around the camellia and at the edge of the root ball. This wrenching will cut through strong roots and encourage others to form nearer the trunk.

The better the preparation for transplanting through wrenching and pruning, the easier it will be to shift a camellia successfully. Most important, however, is the care after lifting. It is critical for roots to be kept covered and moist at all times during lifting and removal. Thorough preparation of the new location, careful planting as soon after lifting as possible and adequate watering are essential. The camellia should be positioned so it is facing in the same direction as it was previously, as there is a danger of severe leaf burn if this is not done.

Chainsaws and bulldozers have been used successfully to transplant very old and well-established camellias, so there is no reason why home gardeners should experience any difficulties, providing careful attention is given to timing, preparation, planting procedures and aftercare.

CHAPTER 5

Landscaping with camellias

There are many and varied landscaping possibilities for camellias in the open ground. They may be grown under other tall trees in a woodland setting, in the open garden or shrubbery, as specimen trees, as standards, as hedging, espaliered, or as ground cover. However they are grouped in the garden, the care of all camellias in the open ground will be as outlined in chapter 4.

Woodland planting

In a large garden with tall trees through which sunshine is filtered, camellias can be planted in a situation that will create something akin to their natural forest habitat. The association with other trees provides shelter and protection in hot, dry summers, as well as some protection from cold weather. The filtered sunlight is less intense, and the loss of water from the soil and from leaves is reduced.

Camellias may grow reasonably well in dense shade but they will not set flower-buds satisfactorily, so trees that create deep shade should be avoided. Deciduous trees are preferable as companions for camellias in a woodland setting, but a combination with other evergreens can be effective. Sufficient space should be allowed between trees to ensure that adequate light reaches the camellias and that nutrients and water are not lost to the marauding roots of other trees.

Fallen leaves will form a blanket of litter, improving growing conditions while contrasting pleasantly with the foliage and brightly coloured blooms of the camellias. Careful selection of shrubs will enhance the planting. Many of the rhododendrons and evergreen azaleas now available would be well suited to the conditions in such a woodland planting.

Opposite: Camellias growing in an open woodland at Heaselands, England.

Two vigorous, upright-growing cultivars that can be used in many different landscaping situations: the black-red, compact 'Midnight' and white, spreading 'Snowman'.

The open garden or shrubbery

Camellias are ideal for providing a background to shrubs, perennials and annuals. They are excellent for hiding an unattractive fence or building, and give height and variation of line to the garden. Perhaps most welcome of all their attributes is their display of blooms at a time when there is little other colour in the garden.

Varieties of camellias can be selected to provide interesting contrasts in size, growth habit, leaf form and texture, and to display colours that harmonise with the garden generally. By selecting varieties with different flowering times, it is possible to have a spectacular garden display over an extended period.

It is important to discuss the most suitable varieties with a local grower or to look at camellias in other gardens. Those listed here are just an introduction; it is impossible to give a complete list. They are grouped according

An attractive garden means colour harmony and contrasting heights and textures. Here, an underplanting of forget-me-nots adds charm to a camellia walk.

'Cinnamon Cindy'

Early:
'Buttons 'n Bows'
'Dream Girl'
'Kathryn Funari'
'Tanya'
'Yuletide'

Early to mid-season:
'Arch of Triumph'
'Aztec'
'Cinnamon Cindy'
'Lois Shinault'
'Margaret Hilford'
'Mark Alan'
'San Dimas'
'Show Girl'
'Spring Mist'
'Tiny Princess'
'Yoi-machi'

Early to late:
'Barbara Clark'
'Nicky Crisp'
'Nymph'
'Snowdrop'
'Takanini'

Mid-season:
'Annette Carol'
'Applause'
'Bellbird'
'Betty's Beauty'
'Contemplation'
'Cornish Snow'
'Debbie'
'Donation'
'Dr Clifford Parks'
'Dream Boat'
'E. G. Waterhouse'
'Fimbriata'
'Freedom Bell'
'Robert Fortune' ('Pagoda')
'Ruby Queen'
'Sanpei-tsubaki'
'San Marino'
'Valentine Day'

Mid-season to late:
'Alpen Glo'
'Arcadia'
'Black Lace'
'Isaribi'
'Jean Pursel'
'Jubilation'
'Night Rider'
'Nonie Haydon'
'Pink Dahlia'
'Spring Festival'

Late:
'Ai-no-izumi'
'Botan-yuki'
'Brian'
'Captain Rawes'
'Harold L. Paige'
'Jingan-cha'
'Mudancha'('Moutancha')

'Captain Rawes' growing as a specimen tree in Kihi Kihi, New Zealand, attracts considerable attention from passing travellers.

Flowering freely for a long time each year, 'Freedom Bell', a vigorous, upright-growing hybrid, can be spectacular as a specimen tree.

to flowering season, but a more refined consideration will take into account colour and growth habit. The time of flowering indicated here is a guide only. The flowering season may be influenced by the weather, and many varieties bloom for a relatively long period.

Varieties suggested for the shrubbery or open garden could also be used as specimen trees and vice versa.

Specimen trees

There are thousands of varieties that can be used to create striking focal points in the garden. The numerous fine specimens, many years old, growing in isolation in New Zealand cemeteries, reserves and farm paddocks, stand testimony to the value of camellias in this role. The only difference in care from those planted in a garden group or shrubbery will be greater spacing to allow the specimen tree to develop to its natural shape.

The majestic *C. reticulata* and its hybrids come into their own as specimen trees. Most of them make a dramatic sight when featured in an open position and allowed to grow freely.

The species *C. tsaii*, *C. rosiflora* and *C. transnokoensis* and tall, upright *C. japonica*, as well as many of the newer hybrids, standing alone or in pairs, will add elegance to a lawn or accent an entrance. A fully developed camellia standing by itself at the end of a long vista of lawn and garden can be a memorable sight.

CAMELLIAS FOR SPECIMEN TREES

C. rosiflora
C. transnokoensis
C. tsaii
'Al Gunn'
'Applause'
'Arcadia'
'Ariel's Song'
'Betty's Beauty'
'Bob Hope'
'Bokuhan' ('Tinsie')
'Cinnamon Cindy'
'Crimson Robe'
'Descanso Mist'
'Donation'
'Dr Clifford Parks'
'Dream Boat'
'Freedom Bell'
'Gwen Washbourne'
'Guilio Nuccio'
'Jubilation'
'Lasca Beauty'
'Margaret Hilford'
'Mary Phoebe Taylor'
'Midnight'
'Mudancha'('Moutancha')
'Nuccio's Ruby'
'Nymph'
'Otome' ('Pink Perfection')
'Robert Fortune' ('Pagoda')
'S. P. Dunn'
'San Dimas'
'Sandy Clark'
'Silver Chalice'
'Silver Cloud'
'Snowdrop'
'Spring Festival'
'Spring Mist'
'Swan Lake'
'Terrell Weaver'
'Valentine Day'
'Wildfire'
'William Hertrich'
'Wirlinga Princess'
'Woodford Harrison'

'Sandy Clark'

'Woodford Harrison'

Standards

Standard forms can add variety and interest to the garden. A camellia standard is created through pruning and training. There are two ways to do this. The first and most straightforward is to select a straight-stemmed, strong-growing plant and cut away all branches and growth from the ground level to the desired height, leaving sufficient top growth to be in balance with the trunk. The top should be pruned to give a pleasing shape.

The second method is to select a strong-growing plant with a straight trunk and graft a preferred variety on to it, well above ground level. Striking effects

CAMELLIAS FOR STANDARDS

'Anticipation'
'Ballet Queen'
'Contemplation'
'Coronation'
'Dolly Dyer'
'E. G. Waterhouse'
'Gayle Walden'
'Grace Albritton'
'Kumagai' (Nagoya)
'Lady Loch'
'Laurie Bray'
'Mary Phoebe Taylor'
'Moshio'
'Spring Festival'
'Yoi-machi'

Most *C. reticulata* cultivars, because of their rapid and open growth habit, can be pruned and trained as tall standards, providing a colourful canopy under which other plants can be grown. Try:
'Barbara Clark'
'Betty Ridley'
'Brian'
'Dr Clifford Parks'
'S. P. Dunn'
'San Marino'
'Terrell Weaver'
'Woodford Harrison'

Weeping or trailing varieties for grafting onto a standard could include:
C. tsaii
'Baby Willow'
'Dave's Weeper'
'Early Pearly'
'Elegant Beauty'
'Hakuhan-kujaku'
'Quintessence'
'Rosiflora Cascade'
'Setsugekka'
'Showa-no-sakae'
'Weeping Maiden'
'Wirlinga Princess'

'Weeping Maiden'

Opposite: 'Spring Festival' will give pleasure in a shrubbery, as a specimen tree or in a container, and is spectacular trained as a standard.

A camellia trained as a standard makes an interesting focal point in the paved area of this garden.

can be achieved by grafting weeping or trailing varieties to the standard. Grafting techniques are detailed on page 153.

Training a standard camellia, particularly in the first few years, will require regular attention. Leaf-buds, which are sure to appear on the stock or trunk, should be removed immediately to prevent any branches developing below the established crown of foliage. Pruning a standard camellia calls for extra care to obtain and maintain the desired shape. While the general principles of removing weak branches and opening up the plant are still important, it is also necessary to shorten some lateral branches to a leaf-bud growing in the direction desired and to pinch back vigorous new growth so that it is not too dominant.

A standard will also need staking to ensure a straight, upright trunk. As the plant grows taller, the new growth of the leader should be tied to the stake at intervals. It will soon develop enough strength to hold its position without restraints.

Hedging

Planting procedures and aftercare for a camellia hedge are the same as for specimens in the open garden, except that they will be planted as close as 1 metre (3 feet) apart or even a little closer. There are two ways of pruning a camellia hedge. Most people follow the traditional practice of tight clipping with shears to give a straight, uniform appearance. The wall of green foliage is attractive and an effective windbreak, but the quality of the flowers will be inferior.

All camellias, including those forming a hedge, benefit from air and light reaching the centre. The most effective pruning of a camellia hedge will follow the same general principles as those set out in chapter 4. The ideal camellia hedge will be more open and informal than the tight, traditional hedge form, and the result will be healthier plants and flowers of better size, form and colour.

When selecting camellias for a mixed-variety hedge, it is preferable to keep to varieties with similar growth habits, although it really depends upon the effect that is wanted. If the preferred hedge is to be of uniform height and rate of growth, plants of the same variety should be chosen. If more informality is sought, a mix of camellias with varying growth habits will be the answer. If the hedge is to act as a screen, it is important to select varieties

Camellias grown as an informal hedge, separating a driveway from another property and acting as a windbreak.

that will grow quickly to the height required—some people will want a very tall windbreak, others will be looking for a hedge about 2 metres (6 feet) tall.

Some thought should also be given to flowering preferences. If a mass of flowers over the entire hedge is the aim, it will be necessary to select either just one variety or several that flower at the same time. A *C. sasanqua* hedge, for example, will give a spectacular display in autumn with a possible bonus of strong fragrance. It is also possible to select a range of varieties that will result in parts of the hedge being in flower over a period of about six months.

CAMELLIAS SUITABLE FOR HEDGING

'Alison Leigh Woodroof'
'Anticipation'
'Barbara Clark'
'Berenice Boddy'
'Bert Jones'
'Bettie Patricia'
'Bonanza'
'Brian'
'Brigadoon'
'Chansonette'
'Choji-guruma'
'Debutante'
'Dixie Knight'
'Donation'
'Elfin Rose'
'Fircone'
'Fire Chief'
'Fire Falls'
'Fukuzutsumi'
'Gay Border'
'Gay Sue'
'Golden Temple' ('Daitairin')
'Grand Slam'
'Jean May'
'Jennifer Susan'
'Jubilation'
'Julia Hamiter'
'Kanjiro'
'Kramer's Supreme'
'Lady Loch'
'Lucinda'
'Misty Moon'
'Otome'
'Phyl Doak'
'Pink Pagoda'
'Plantation Pink'
'Setsugekka'
'Shishi-gashira'
'Showa-no-sakae'
'Sunset Glory'
'Tanya'
'Yuletide'

A formal hedge of 'Kanjiro'

'Bert Jones' (left), semi-double, and 'Bettie Patricia', rose-form double, are both *C. sasanqua* cultivars suitable for hedging or for training as an informal espalier.

C. sasanqua cultivars trained against a trellis as an informal espalier.

Espalier

'Espalier' is from the French word for trellis. It has been adopted in English horticultural language to describe a plant trained to grow two-dimensionally (to be espaliered) against a trellis or wall.

Espaliers are an excellent way for the collector to include more varieties in a small area. More importantly, they are an effective means of making a trellis attractive, hiding an unsightly fence or wall, or screening one section of the garden from another. This is also a useful technique for training camellias over an arch or pergola. 'Elegant Beauty', for example, is eminently suited to this, for it can be easily controlled in either a formal or informal pattern. It will soon cover the required area with attractive foliage and be a real joy when flowering.

Any situation is suitable for an espalier, with the proviso that the intensity of heat should be considered. A solid, concrete or block wall facing the sun will reflect undue heat unless something is done to reduce its effect. Securing a close wooden trellis may eliminate the problem.

If the espalier is to be against a solid wall, it will be necessary to provide wires to which the branches can be tied. Alternatively, wooden slats may be fixed to the wall, or rows of garden twine may be stretched from end to end

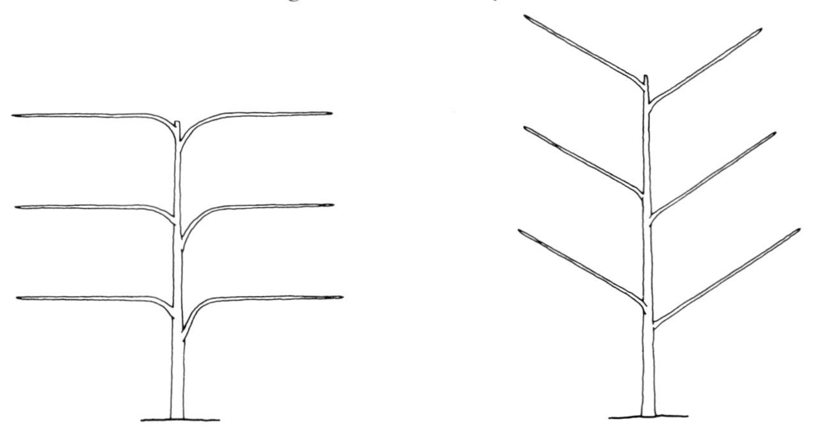

The branches of an espaliered camellia can be trained to grow either horizontally (left) or at an angle (right) from a single leading stem.

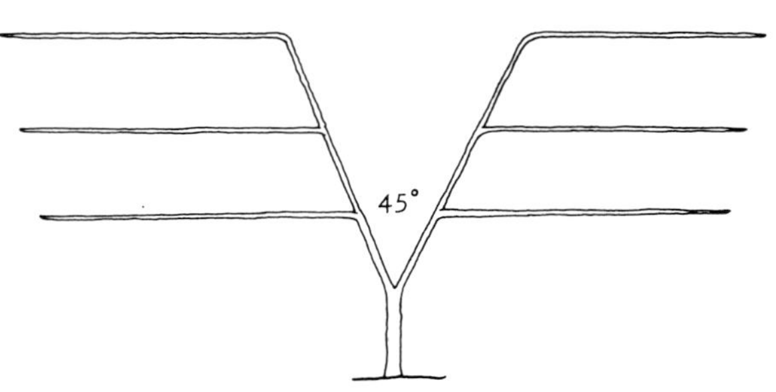

Alternatively, two or more leaders can be arranged symmetrically and lateral branches from these trained horizontally.

and used to train the branches. The twine should last long enough for the branches to strengthen sufficiently to hold their position without support. Whatever the method used, it should be arranged with air circulation around and behind the branches.

Developing the ideal espalier takes time and patience but is an easy exercise if the desired result is visualised from the beginning. Espaliers will usually be shaped in one of two basic patterns. From a central leading stem,

'Donation' espaliered in the Bodnant gardens, North Wales, a reminder that any camellia can be trained in this way.

branches may be trained to grow either horizontally or at an angle, parallel to each other. Alternatively, two or more leaders starting from near the base may be arranged symmetrically. Lateral branches from these may then be trained horizontally.

The most suitable varieties to espalier are those with a natural willowy or sprawling habit of growth. Most sasanquas are ideal, but many other cultivars are also suitable. In fact, any camellia can be espaliered, though controlling and training some varieties will involve considerable work. Having selected and planted a suitable specimen, following the same procedures as for any other camellia in the open ground, the leaders should be tied to the support and any growth that is not required should be removed. Soft ties, plastic or twine, are preferable; wire should be avoided as it may cut into the branch. As the plant grows, the leader and laterals should be tied in the desired positions and unwanted stems and branches removed.

Cut off any branches and rub off leaf-buds that will lead to growth downwards or to the rear, and remove any other growth that interferes with the development of the pattern. The main pruning of espaliers should be done, as with other camellias, at the end of the flowering season and before the flush of new spring growth. Regular, selective training will make this task much easier and keep the espalier attractive at all times.

Each year the espaliered camellias will present a fine display of blooms, for in this method of cultivation flowers cannot be hidden from sight.

CAMELLIAS SUITABLE FOR ESPALIER

'Alpen Glo'

- 'Alpen Glo'
- 'Ariel's Song'
- 'Bonanza'
- 'Cornish Snow'
- 'Coronation'
- 'Dave's Weeper'
- 'Donation'
- 'Elegant Beauty'
- 'Fukuzutsumi'
- 'Hakuhan-kujaku'
- 'Jennifer Susan'
- 'Lucinda'
- 'Mine-no-yuki'
- 'Nymph'
- 'Our Melissa'
- 'Plantation Pink'
- 'Setsugekka'
- 'Sparkling Burgundy'
- 'Taishuhai'
- 'Tama-no-ura'

Ground cover

Slow-growing camellias or those with a sprawling growth habit can be used to good effect as ground covers. Slow-growing varieties, planted as an edging in front of larger camellias, or grouped under them, can be impressive. Willowy-branched or sprawling sasanquas and similar species and hybrids can be trained to grow like a horizontal espalier, under other plants and on banks. Plants should be encouraged to grow horizontally just above ground level, through selective pruning to promote side growth.

Plants can be kept growing a few centimetres above the ground by means of U-shaped wires pressed into the ground, or by tying branches at intervals to stakes.

CAMELLIAS FOR GROUND COVER

'Baby Bear' (front) and 'Nicky Crisp'

'Fairy Wand'

Slow-growing:
'Baby Bear'
'Baby Willow'
'Black Opal'
'Bonsai Baby'
'Gwen Pike'
'Itty Bit'
'Nicky Crisp'
'Pink Cameo'
'Reigyoku'
'Snippet'
'The Elf'
'Twilight'

Although all are slow-growing, they differ in other characteristics. For example, in one situation the dwarf 'Baby Bear' may be preferred, while in another, the upright 'Nicky Crisp' may be more appropriate.

Open-growing:
'Elegant Beauty'
'Fairy Wand'
'Mine-no-yuki'
'Nymph'
'Plantation Pink'
'Shishi-gashira'
'Showa-no-sakae'
'Tama-no-ura'
and others suggested for espalier.

The slow-growing, floriferous 'Itty Bit' can be effective grown as a ground cover in front of more vigorous varieties.

'Tomorrow Park Hill' grown as a standard with plants of the dwarf 'Baby Bear' as a surrounding ground cover.

Several outstanding camellias have been omitted from the above lists because, although they have spectacular flowers, they do not display them to make a great splash of colour in the garden. 'Tiffany', for example, produces many near-perfect flowers because they hang downwards, giving themselves protection. Planted on a bank so that the blooms can be viewed from below, 'Tiffany' is a wonderful sight. Members of the 'Elegans' family—'Elegans Champagne', 'Elegans Supreme' and 'Elegans Splendor'—also have exhibition-quality flowers but do not always do themselves justice as garden plants because the flowers face downwards. These camellias will always give pleasure, but their location should be carefully chosen. Excellent display blooms can be picked from any of them, and they are worth growing for this attribute alone.

Companion plants

As beautiful as the camellia is, a garden composed only of camellias would lack real character. The aim of most gardeners is to have beauty in the garden through all seasons, and this can be achieved readily by establishing other

Opposite: Many other plants grow well with camellias. Here, a silver border enriches the vivid reds of the camellias.

plants with camellias to give variation in height and foliage, and harmonious combinations of colour and texture.

There is a vast range of plants that will harmonise with the handsome green foliage and autumn-through-winter flowering of camellias. Providing that the plants chosen are tolerant of the same soil conditions as camellias, favourite annuals, perennials and shrubs can be planted among and under the camellias. However, care must be taken to avoid a clash of colours when a companion flowers at the same time as a nearby camellia. This can happen if enthusiasm is not tempered with a little discretion and planning. A burst of bright orange near a pink camellia may destroy all efforts to achieve beauty and harmony.

Several factors may be considered in the selection of companion plants. Are trees and shrubs needed to provide shelter and shade? Should they be selected to complement the camellias in flower or to add interest when the flowering season is over? Which small plants will provide contrast and colour nearer the ground level?

As azaleas and rhododendrons prefer acid conditions, they are likely to thrive in a garden that suits camellias. Nandina, gardenia and oleander can also fit in well with camellias. Fuchsia, daphne and varieties of pieris can add to the charm of the garden. Other trees will give a different accent to the planting. Magnolia species, such as *M. denudata* or *M. soulangeana*, can look magnificent when planted in association with camellias.

There are numerous border and ground-cover plants that will add variety to the camellia garden. Hostas will thrive and provide complementary foliage. Ground covers like ajuga, liriope and muscari can be useful. However, a word of warning must be given about invasive, ground-covering plants near young camellias. Plants with tight root systems, such as pratia or violets, are likely to grow between the roots of young camellias as they try to establish themselves, hindering their development. Lilies, daylilies, daisies and bulbs of all sorts can add variety. Ferns will also be enhanced by the camellia background, and there is a place for climbers such as clematis.

It would not be helpful to present a long list of plants that might be grown with camellias. You should discover from the local nursery or botanic gardens which plants grow well in your area. Then, when planning for the overall effect, select those that will thrive in free-draining, slightly acid soil containing considerable organic matter.

CHAPTER 6

Camellias in containers

Throughout its history as an ornamental plant, the camellia has been grown in containers. There are reports of tree-sized plants in tubs in the courtyards of early Buddhist monasteries in China, and the ancient dwarfed bonsai camellias of Japan are well known. The value of growing camellias in containers has also been recognised in the Western world for many years.

Though more careful attention must be given to the aftercare of camellias in containers than is necessary with those in the open ground, there are many benefits. In modern, urban homes with little outdoor space, as well as in large gardens, camellias in containers can provide beauty and variety. Proper care and attention may bring earlier and better-quality flowers on container plants than those produced by the same varieties in the ground. The greatest advantage, though, is the ability to move the containers about, placing them to create the greatest impact at entranceways, on paved areas, patios and terraces, or perhaps on walls. Camellias that have finished flowering can be changed for ones that are just beginning.

In the extreme conditions of some regions, camellias in containers may need to spend winter months in the warmth of greenhouses and be moved outside for the summer. Even in more favourable climates, the effects of unseasonable winds or severe storms can be avoided through this mobility. In hotter regions, containerised camellias can be moved into the shade during the hottest part of the day.

Container growing can be a boon to the enthusiastic collector of camellia varieties, allowing for a large number of plants in a small area.

Pots and tubs

Containers come in a range of shapes, sizes and materials, including wood, porous terra cotta or earthenware, impervious plastic or glazed ceramics, concrete or metal. Different materials will create different conditions for the

Container-grown camellias brighten a
Chinese courtyard.

plant, particularly the container's ability to retain moisture or withstand either frosts or heat. If all containers are made of the same material, care is more straightforward, as it is easier to determine the plant's needs. Most containers used today are made from glazed or unglazed earthenware, plastic or timber. Unlike the others, glazed earthenware and plastic pots will not lose any water through their sides and will require less water. However, plastic containers will absorb heat more readily than others and need some protection from the sun. In areas of severe frost, there is some danger of the roots of container-grown camellias becoming frozen. Plastic containers are likely to be most at risk, though earthenware ones may crack in an extreme frost.

With both glazed and unglazed earthenware pots, features that are appealing may not be desirable. Some of the most attractive of these containers are narrower at the top than in the middle, and should be avoided because of the difficulties in removing the plant for repotting. As the roots develop, they spread in the container to fill the space, and it may be necessary to break the pot to be able to remove the plant with the root ball intact. For this reason, a container that is slightly tapered towards the bottom is preferable to any other, including one with straight sides.

There is sometimes a danger that the beauty and style of the container may become the focal point and detract from the plant. Always select one that will be unobtrusive, with a neutral colour that will blend with and show off the plant to best effect.

Whatever type of pot or tub is preferred, the size must be sufficient to allow the root system to develop and grow. However, it is important to avoid placing a very small plant in a large container. A small camellia is best planted in a container that allows no more than about 5 cm (2 in.) of free potting mixture right around the root system, as the unused soil mix in a container beyond the reach of the roots may become stagnant and harm the plant. As the plant grows, it should be moved each year to a slightly bigger pot, allowing a similar space for root development, until it has reached an appropriate size for a permanent container.

The size of the container finally used will depend upon its purpose and location, as well as the growth habit of the chosen variety. For most camellias, it does not have to be very large. The depth needs to be only about two-thirds of, or the same as, the diameter but it can be greater. A container about 35–40 cm (14–16 in.) across the top and 30–35 cm at the bottom (12–14 in.), with a depth about the same as the top diameter, will be satisfactory.

The container must have efficient drainage, with holes either in the bottom or low down on the sides so that surplus water is eliminated in about 15 minutes. If the drainage is inadequate and this surplus is not cleared quickly, the soggy soil will stagnate, preventing aeration of the roots, and chemicals in the soil will build up to dangerous levels. The camellia will not grow, the leaves will turn yellow and begin to fall off and, if the condition is not corrected quickly, the plant will die. Being too wet is worse than being too dry. If the only drainage holes are in the bottom, the container should be raised slightly above the ground level to facilitate seepage.

Camellias in shadehouses are most frequently grown in containers. Here, 'Mudancha' and 'Julia Hamiter' flower freely.

Planting

Meticulous care must be taken with camellias in containers if they are to flourish. Water and nutrients must be readily available, and good potting mix should be used. Ordinary garden soil will pack too tightly to be of any use.

Commercial potting mix from a reputable company, available from a garden centre, will be satisfactory. It is composed mainly of bark and includes a slow-release fertiliser. Experienced growers tend to make their own potting mix—and there are probably as many different recipes for potting mix as there are growers. Mixes should consist of plenty of organic matter, material that will hold moisture, and material that will create an open soil, allowing space for air around the roots. Ingredients can include bark, untreated sawdust, compost, peat, sand, pumice, vermiculite and perlite. Use peat sparingly, as it breaks down quickly and may hold too much water. All organic material should be well composted before use in a potting mixture, but if any non-rotted organic material is included, it is important that nitrogenous fertiliser such as blood and bone is added. A slow-release fertiliser is very beneficial, and a handful of dolomite lime, particularly when the mix is mostly compost and bark, will improve the pH level and make magnesium available. Either of the following recipes should give pleasing results:

The impact of 'Spring Festival' (left) and *C. transnokoensis* (right) in full bloom can be appreciated when they are planted in tubs and can be moved for effect.

The fragrant, slow-growing and spreading 'Quintessence' is an ideal subject for a container.

Potting mix 1:
Equal quantities of fine (10 mm/0.4 in.) bark, compost or high-quality garden soil, and coarse pumice.

Potting mix 2:
2 parts untreated sawdust, 1 part peat, 1 part high-fibre compost, 2 parts leaf mould, 2 parts bark (10–25 mm/0.4–1 in.), 2 parts coarse pumice.

A handful of a slow-release fertiliser and a small handful of dolomite lime could be added to each mixture.

Ensure that the container is thoroughly clean and that the camellia to be planted in it has been well watered. Make sure also that the ingredients in the potting mix have been combined thoroughly.

Crocks or stones are not necessary at the bottom of the container, but it is desirable to cover the drainage holes with gauze. Several centimetres of the mix should be placed in the bottom of the container and made firm. The depth of mix should allow the root crown of the plant to sit about 5 cm (2 in.) below the top of the container to permit effective watering.

With the plant in position in the centre, the sides can be filled with mix and pressed down. Make sure that the camellia is not buried more deeply

Both 'Black Lace', with its dark, velvet-red flowers, and 'Tammia', which has white flowers with pink centres and borders, are attractive when grown in a container.

than it was in its planter bag. Water the plant thoroughly and allow any surplus to drain away. When the mix has settled, it may be necessary to fill any gaps.

Mulching

Mulching is perhaps even more important for a camellia in a container than it is for one in the ground, as changes in temperature can affect a container-grown camellia drastically. Direct sunlight should be kept off the sides of containers, particularly if they are dark in colour, as the very high temperatures that can build up around the roots in hot weather could kill the plant. A mulch will help to insulate the roots against such change. Whatever is used, it should allow water to pass through it easily and it should prevent the growth of weeds.

Materials suggested for mulching plants in the open ground (page 80) can also be used for containers, to a depth of 2–3 cm (1 in.). It may be desirable to use something that will be permanent as well as attractive, and something that will not be a popular scratching place for birds. Stones, small rocks or pebbles can be useful; so too can the shells of walnuts or any other nuts that are available and, if you collect great quantities of seed from your camellias, their husks. A living mulch or ground cover provided by small plants is another possibility.

Watering

It is essential that watering be thorough and that the soil never be allowed to dry out completely. The location of the containers will affect the frequency of watering. Those exposed to sun and wind will demand more frequent attention than others. A thorough soaking when required will be more beneficial than frequent light sprinklings. As with camellias in the open ground, spraying the leaves in the evening can reduce temperatures, increase humidity and discourage insect pests.

Feeding

Nutrients will leach out more quickly from a container than they would in the open ground, so the plant's supply of nutrients should be replenished regularly. Slow-release fertilisers added at the time of planting are beneficial for the first few months. More of these can be spread under the mulch later. Alternatively, a small quantity of the fertiliser used for camellias in the open ground can be mixed into the topsoil of the container and watered well.

While it is important to repeat the warning about over-fertilising because of the danger to the plant from an undue build-up of salts, it is also worth noting that many container-grown camellias are under-fed. Once again, careful observation is important. Regular spraying with a weak solution of a liquid fertiliser is an easy procedure with beneficial results, as nutrients are absorbed not only through the leaves but also through the roots.

Pruning and disbudding

The principles and guidelines set out in chapter 4 also apply here.

Repotting

If proper care is taken at the time of planting and followed by careful watering and feeding, a camellia can happily remain in its container for a considerable time. Eventually, however, it will become rootbound in the restricted area and will require repotting.

The deteriorating appearance of a plant will soon show that repotting is overdue; try to do it before this stage is reached—approximately every two years. The best time for repotting is towards the end of the flowering season, before the new spring growth begins. If hot weather and this period of very active growth are avoided, repotting can, with care, be carried out at any time.

Remove the plant carefully from the container. With a sharp knife, cut through the root system, removing about 5 cm (2 in.) all round and from the bottom. This will encourage new root growth, which will result in new foliage and better flowers, and will help prevent the plant becoming rootbound. Water the plant thoroughly and put it back in its container with new potting mix. With the root area now reduced, it is wise also to compensate for this loss by pruning to reduce the foliage by about a third.

Any camellia can be grown in a container, but the slower, more compact-growing varieties are easier to handle. Camellias with a weeping habit are very effective in containers.

CAMELLIAS SUITABLE FOR CONTAINERS

'Adorable'

Upright growth:
C. transnokoensis
'Cinnamon Cindy'
'Spring Festival'

Compact-growing:
C. lutchuensis Formosan form
C. pitardii
'Adorable'
'Ave Maria'
'Baby Bear'
'Black Lace'
'Black Opal'
'Demi-Tasse'
'Fimbriata'
'Glen 40'
'Grace Caple'
'Itty Bit'
'Kuro-tsubaki'
'Little Babe'
'Minimint'
'Nicky Crisp'
'Night Rider'
'Prudence'
'Scented Gem'
'Snippet'
'Sugar Babe'
'Tammia'
'Tanya'
'The Elf'
'Tootsie'
'Yuletide'

Weeping or open growth:
C. lutchuensis
'Annette Carol'
'Baby Willow'
'Dresden China'
'Garnet Gleam'
'Our Melissa'
'Persuasion'
'Quintessence'
'Rosiflora Cascade'
'Snowdrop'
'Spring Mist'
'Tama-no-ura',
'Tiny Princess'
'Tiny Star'
'Wirlinga Gem'
'Wirlinga Princess'

Hanging baskets and window boxes

Camellias can be successfully grown in hanging baskets, but again the container should be selected carefully. If a wire basket is to be used, it should be a large one, at least 30 cm (12 in.) wide at the top. Some baskets made of wooden slats, used for smaller plants, may not be big enough or sturdy enough for a camellia. If wood is the preferred material, a reasonably light but strong timber can be chosen to construct a container about 30 cm (12 in.) square at the top and about 15–17 cm (6–7 in.) deep. Whatever is chosen should allow for adequate development of the root system but should not be too heavy.

The principles of planting and aftercare are the same for these camellias as for any others in containers. However, as the branches develop they can be trained by using ties or wires and with careful pruning to create the desired shape. As these containers are intended to hang above head height, the aim is to restrict upwards growth and encourage a cascading effect. With wire baskets, the branches can be tied down easily; with wooden containers, staples may need to be driven in low down and the ties attached to these. Copper wire can also be used, twisted around a young branch and bent to the desired position. If the branches are trained when they are young and supple, they will soon adapt to what is required. For a time the ties will need adjusting, but as the plant grows stronger they can be removed. The regular

Any camellia with open or weeping growth, particularly if it has small flowers and leaves, will be attractive when trained in a hanging basket.

removal of unwanted growth will maintain an attractive plant.

Growing camellias in window boxes is not a common practice, but there are many varieties that can provide a colourful display in this way. The same principles of selection, care and training as for hanging baskets can be followed.

Camellias with miniature or small flowers and small leaves are particularly suitable for growing in a hanging basket or window box. They will be most effective if they have a weeping or spreading growth habit. Members of the 'Elegans' group are attractive, despite their large flowers.

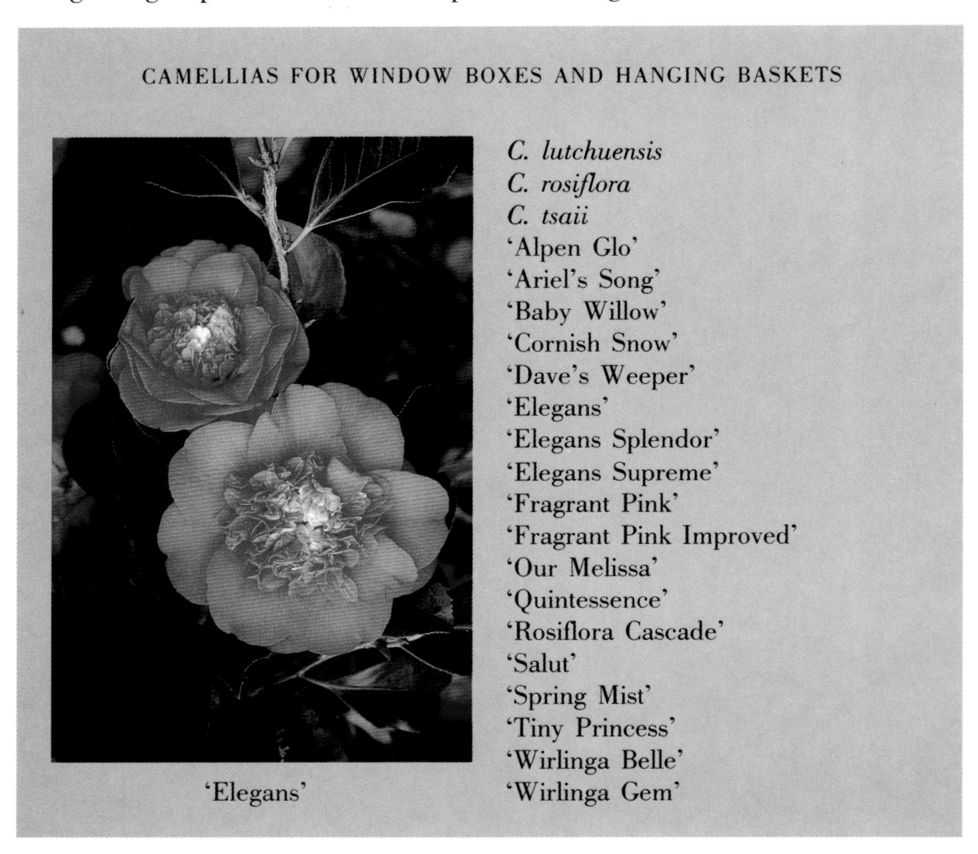

CAMELLIAS FOR WINDOW BOXES AND HANGING BASKETS

C. lutchuensis
C. rosiflora
C. tsaii
'Alpen Glo'
'Ariel's Song'
'Baby Willow'
'Cornish Snow'
'Dave's Weeper'
'Elegans'
'Elegans Splendor'
'Elegans Supreme'
'Fragrant Pink'
'Fragrant Pink Improved'
'Our Melissa'
'Quintessence'
'Rosiflora Cascade'
'Salut'
'Spring Mist'
'Tiny Princess'
'Wirlinga Belle'
'Wirlinga Gem'

'Elegans'

Bonsai

Bonsai originated in China, perhaps more than 500 years BC. The art later became popular in Japan, and it is to these countries that bonsai growers in the western world look for inspiration. The word bonsai means literally, 'plant in a tray', and it will remain just that unless it is trained artistically in the tradition of bonsai.

In classical bonsai a seedling may be forced to develop a bent and twisted tap-root by growing it in a pot with alternate layers of pebbles and sand. This seedling is used as understock, and a desired variety is grafted onto it. Alter-

'Baby Bear', with its small flowers and leaves, is very suitable for training in the bonsai form.

natively, a large, old, crooked root found on an unwanted camellia can be used as an understock. A smaller scion is grafted onto this stock, and the branches and foliage are trained to a typical bonsai shape, giving the appearance of great age and beauty. The gnarled and twisted trunk accentuates the freshness and clear lines of the branches and foliage, with the mass of blooms adding to the striking effect.

Anyone who wishes to grow camellias, or any other plant, as miniatures in the bonsai style should read a book on the subject. Several are available in public libraries and some are listed in the bibliography on page 171. It would also be worthwhile joining a bonsai society. A member of the local camellia society may be a keen exponent of bonsai and willing to help a beginner. The barest outline of basic requirements and care are given here.

Containers for bonsai

Bonsai pots come in a variety of shapes and sizes. The size of the pot in relation to the size of the tree is important. A pot whose length is about two-thirds the height of the tree seems to be the right proportion. A relatively deep pot is most appropriate for a tree with a thick trunk, while shallower pots better suit more slender trees. The shape and colour of the pot are a matter of personal preference. Although brown is a safe colour to choose, the glossy, green foliage of a camellia may look its best in a blue or green pot. As with other containers, a bonsai pot must have large drainage holes.

Selecting a camellia for bonsai

Two approaches can be followed:

1. Young seedlings may be grown on to a stage where they have a strong leader with several branches and are suitable for planting in an ornamental bonsai pot. Seedlings may be found growing under established camellia trees or produced from seed (see chapter 8). In either case, the tap-root should be shortened to about half of its length, or less, to encourage the growth of fibrous roots.

2. Alternatively, a small but mature plant may be obtained, repotted and trained as a bonsai. The best ones for the purpose may possibly be found discarded at the nursery because they are a shape that is unsuitable for the ordinary garden but suggests great possibilities for bonsai.

A camellia about 25–30 cm (10–12 in.) tall with a trunk that is very wide at the base and with a good number of branches low down will be ideal to work with. Once a plant has been obtained, it should be grown on in a planter bag or pot and shaped in preparation for transferring the following year to its bonsai container.

Virtually all camellia species and varieties may be trained as bonsai, but some will be more appropriate for achieving the desired final result. The plant should be small when selected, with its shape influencing the final decision. Look for one that has an interesting twist to its trunk or some other feature that can be trained into an attractive form.

Some of the species with their small flowers and small leaves are ideal for bonsai, but so too are many of the newer hybrids, like 'Itty Bit' or 'Cinnamon Cindy'. Some may appeal, not only because of their beautiful flowers and foliage, but also because of their growth habit. The naturally dwarf 'Baby Bear', the slow-growing, 'Nicky Crisp' and 'Snippet', or a willowy sasanqua

Young camellias being trained as bonsai.

The growth habit and flower form of both 'Kuro-tsubaki' (left) and 'Yoi-machi' make them excellent subjects for bonsai.

like 'Mine-no-yuki' trained in a weeping style can be very effective. Camellias with bigger flowers and leaves can be developed as larger bonsai in deeper pots.

Soil mix

Like other camellia growers, bonsai enthusiasts have their own preferences for a potting mix. It must satisfy the requirements of including adequate nutrients and retaining moisture, but should provide good drainage to remove excess water quickly and allow aeration.

A commercial mix could be used, or a mixture made up of equal parts of loam or topsoil, peat or compost, and coarse river sand. The qualities of the mix should be observed after heavy watering, noting its ability to absorb moisture and to drain any excess water. At the same time check that the soil surface has not caked hard. Adjustments should be made to the mix to achieve the best possible performance. Fine metal chips or coarse pumice might improve moisture retention as well as aeration and drainage. Remember too that the camellia prefers a soil that is slightly acid. The inclusion of more peat or compost can help to provide this. Slow-release fertilisers in the soil mix will provide the nutrients needed for some months.

Potting

1. Clean the bonsai pot and cover the drainage holes with fine plastic mesh, copper or stainless steel gauze.

2. Place a level layer of the soil mix in the pot on top of a sprinkling of small gravel.

3. Carefully remove the plant from its temporary container and wash the soil from its roots. One knowledgeable bonsai enthusiast recommends standing the root ball in a bucket of water containing one crushed vitamin B1 tablet, or one tablespoon of vitamin B1 compound, before preparing the root system for planting. Most of the soil will fall away, the rest can be carefully removed and the roots pruned. The vitamin acts immediately, alleviating shock and acting as a growth hormone.

4. Cut off most of the tap-root and reduce the root system to about two-thirds of the length and width of the bonsai pot.

5. Place the tree in the pot with its base visible at eye level. Fill around it and over its roots with new dry soil and make it firm.

6. Water it thoroughly without disturbing the soil. This can be done easily by standing it in another dish containing water reaching nearly to the top of the bonsai pot.

7. Keep the bonsai in a shady place for two to three weeks, with protection from strong winds and heavy rain.

Fertiliser

Regular feeding in small amounts is desirable, and under-feeding is preferable to over-feeding. Strong, green leaves will indicate a healthy plant. With compost in the mix supplying most, if not all, of the nutrients necessary, there will be little need for additional feeding in between repottings, although an occasional weak foliage spray is beneficial. A slow-release fertiliser could be added when potting or repotting.

Watering

This is essential. A fine spray of water will benefit the foliage as well as soaking the soil. In the growing season and throughout summer, daily watering will be needed. If there is no rain, this should be done in the early morning or in the evening when the sun is not shining on the leaves.

During a dry spell, as well as regular watering, it is sound practice to plunge the whole container into a tray of water, deep enough to cover the soil, and leave it until bubbles stop rising.

Placement

Somewhere free of strong winds, cold draughts and very strong sunshine will benefit the bonsai. Three or four hours of sunshine is ideal, in a place that will enable the plant to benefit from any rainfall. Common sense should be the guiding factor in placing the bonsai in summer and winter, according to local conditions.

Pruning and shaping

Constant pinching of twigs or removal of leaf-buds will help to establish and maintain the desired shape. Most camellias will be grown in an informal, upright style. Heavier branches may be removed when the plant has finished flowering.

Though copper wire may be twisted around branches to achieve the shape and position sought, it is preferable to use a soft material to tie branches down in the preferred position. If wire is used, it can be removed when the branch is sufficiently mature to retain the position.

Repotting

A bonsai camellia needs to be repotted only when it is starting to become pot-bound, probably two or more years later. With the plant out of the pot, about one-third of the soil from the top and sides can be removed and all exposed roots cut off. Another third of the soil can be removed from the bottom and exposed roots cut off before replanting with new soil and slow-release fertiliser, and watering.

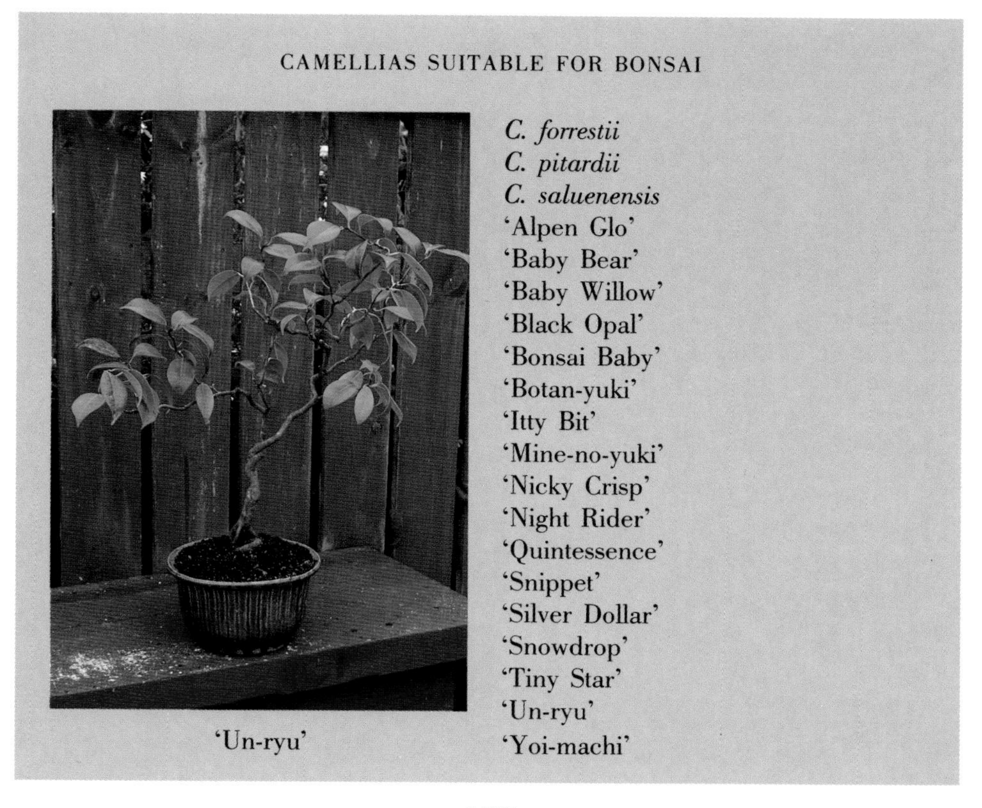

CAMELLIAS SUITABLE FOR BONSAI

C. forrestii
C. pitardii
C. saluenensis
'Alpen Glo'
'Baby Bear'
'Baby Willow'
'Black Opal'
'Bonsai Baby'
'Botan-yuki'
'Itty Bit'
'Mine-no-yuki'
'Nicky Crisp'
'Night Rider'
'Quintessence'
'Snippet'
'Silver Dollar'
'Snowdrop'
'Tiny Star'
'Un-ryu'
'Yoi-machi'

'Un-ryu'

CHAPTER 7

Disorders, diseases and pests

Observation is the starting point in dealing with any disorders, diseases or pests. If symptoms can be recognised at an early stage, the problem can often be minimised. The healthier plants are, the less likely they are to suffer from the ravages of insect pests or fungal diseases. Care in planting, including the provision of adequate drainage, and attention to cultural practices such as pruning and mulching, will do much to ensure that plants thrive. It should be a standard procedure to review all cultural practices whenever there are concerns about the well-being of camellias.

This discussion of disorders, diseases and pests is not exhaustive but does include the most likely ones encountered.

Disorders

Physiological disorders may result from climatic changes, nutritional imbalances (usually deficiencies) or poor care (such as failure to provide adequate drainage or to water sufficiently, or over-feeding with chemical fertiliser). If a young plant looks unhealthy for no identifiable reason, scratch away some soil from around the roots or lift the plant to have a close look at the root system. White roots are a sign of health below the ground, but dull brown and rotting roots mean that something, probably drainage, is wrong. Correcting the drainage and careful replanting, perhaps in another position, may solve the problem.

Algae and lichen

Algae may appear on the leaves of camellias growing in shady but humid positions. Though unattractive, this dull green growth has no effect on the health of the plant except that severe deposits prevent light reaching the leaf. Improving the light available and opening up the plant by pruning will be beneficial. Spraying with copper oxychloride should reduce the incidence of algae. Soapy water with white oil sprayed alternately with copper mixtures has also proved effective.

Lichen, although it has no effect on the performance of a camellia, may be unsightly and perhaps harbour insect pests. Some growers believe that lichen becomes established on plants that are less healthy than they should be and suggest that action should be taken to encourage more vigour in the plant. Spraying with copper oxychloride (50%) should kill lichen but it will be firmly attached and stay on the tree for a long time unless loosened by vigorous brushing.

Browned petals

Camellias with white and pale pink flowers may develop brown petals from exposure to sun or wind. The more delicate-coloured varieties, in particular, will benefit from some protection from extremes of weather. Judicious pruning to prevent blooms from rubbing against other parts of the plant will do much to prevent browning caused by the wind.

One technique used by many growers in the United States to avoid the worst effects of cold weather, which may also cause browned petals, is to encourage early blooming and a longer flowering season by applying gibberellic acid to developing flower-buds. Treated blooms are larger than normal, which is also seen by some as an advantage. It is claimed that without this practice camellia growing as a hobby would not be possible in some areas. Using gibberellic acid is considered to be unnecessary in New Zealand, and the procedure is generally frowned upon. Blooms treated in this way would not be permitted in New Zealand shows.

Bud drop

Occasionally, flower-buds will fall without opening. This may happen when a plant develops very large clusters of buds. With young camellias, particularly reticulatas, it may be due to frosty conditions. Extreme changes of temperature may be a cause with any variety.

If bud drop occurs year after year, all cultural practices should be checked thoroughly. It may be necessary to move the plant to another position, perhaps a cooler spot, out of the direct sunlight.

Some older varieties—'Lady St. Clair' was a notorious offender—caused growers great anguish with their propensity for flower-buds to 'ball' and fail to open. The tendency of some cultivars to do this has been recognised and they have disappeared from the market.

Chlorosis

Yellowing of the leaves, known as chlorosis, may have any one of several causes. The leaves of a camellia have a life span of about three years and will become discoloured before falling to the ground. Yellowing may be due to a genetic or inherited condition. If so, the yellow markings on the leaves will be regular in shape and arrangement. Other yellowing may be caused by a virus (see page 134).

General yellowing or blanching of the leaves associated with the loss of chlorophyll may follow an extended dry period with insufficient water, or an excess of water with poor drainage. If the situation is not remedied quickly, the plant is likely to drop its leaves, stop growing and finally die.

Another cause of chlorosis may be excessive alkalinity of the soil, a high pH level, preventing some nutrients such as iron from being available in a soluble form. Provided that the drainage is efficient, this condition may be remedied by the application of iron chelate or the less effective sulphate of iron. Compost and/or the use of so-called 'acid' fertilisers could also help.

Yellowing surrounding green veins may indicate a lack of either iron or magnesium. This can readily be corrected by the application of sulphate of iron or magnesium sulphate (Epsom salts), or a small quantity of dolomite lime. A general fertiliser with trace elements, or spraying with liquid blood and bone containing trace elements, should also bring a quick return of colour and renewed vigour. Remember to apply fertilisers in small quantities at a time.

Corky or leaf scab

Over-watering or irregular watering may cause plants to absorb more water through the roots than the leaves can transpire, a condition known as oedema. This results in blisters on the undersides of the leaves, which burst and harden into scabs. It can occur with camellias that have a large root system and relatively little foliage.

Chlorosis

Corky or leaf scab

Dieback

Leaf burn or scorch

Some cultivars in a hot, sunny position may suffer from sunburn, with brown or bronze patches on the leaves. A move from direct sunshine or the provision of some protection will help avoid this. Sunburn on upper leaf surfaces is also a symptom of potash deficiency and can be corrected by the use of 30 per cent potassic superphosphate.

If the edges of leaves are brown, it is likely that there has been an excessive build-up of salts in the soil, perhaps as a result of over-fertilising. This can usually be corrected by a thorough watering to wash the salts from the immediate root zone.

Diseases

Camellias are generally free from disease, but in every country there are pathogens that thrive in the local environment and manifest themselves when conditions suit them. Although most home gardeners will never see signs of disease in their camellias, the most important preventive action is to follow cultural procedures carefully and to develop strong-growing, healthy plants. These will be less likely to be affected and better able to resist disease.

Dieback

Dieback caused by the fungus *Glomerella cingulata* can be lethal to camellias. The disease is first seen as a sudden wilting and death of young shoots (the twig blight phase). Dead leaves then become dark brown and hold on to the shoot. This is followed by the dying of tissue and the growth of a canker (the canker stage). If undetected cankers on the trunk or branches

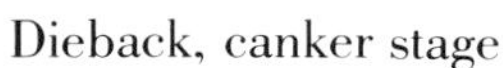
Dieback, canker stage

Leaf gall

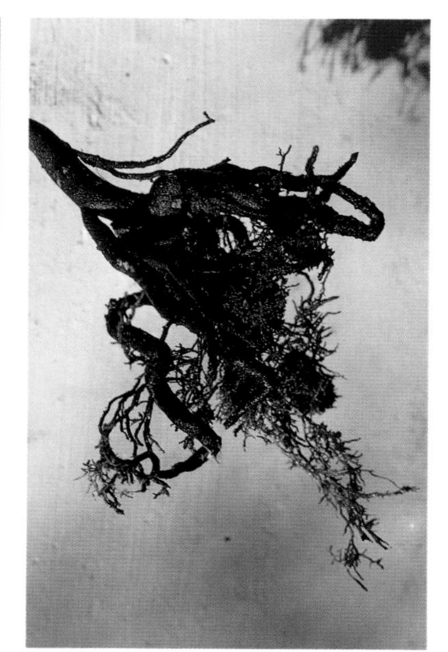

Root rot

continue to enlarge, water and nutrients will not reach the branch tops and the result will be a yellowing of leaves, loss of foliage and dieback of twigs and branches. Signs of *Glomerella* should be looked for when purchasing a plant.

The infection can enter the plant through a wound when conditions are warm and humid. Note, in the section on pruning, how branch rings and collars should be left undamaged to prevent the entry of pathogens. Infection is more likely to occur when plants are crowded, with poor circulation of air, or are in dense shade or have inadequate drainage.

There is always the possibility that a plant affected by dieback will die. The disease is more likely to occur in warmer climates and is a major concern for plant exporters and those who grow camellias in glasshouses. Any infected plant material, including discoloured wood and branches, should be removed and burnt. The area should then be treated with a fungicide. It may be helpful to prune the plant at the same time.

Leaf gall

Exobasidium spp., common in other countries and recently identified in New Zealand, is a wind-borne fungus affecting leaves when they are very small. The leaves become very thick and much bigger than they would be normally. They may be light green or white in colour but sometimes take on a deep pink or reddish appearance. They are very prominent and ugly, and always at the end of branches.

When leaf gall is noticed, other leaves will be too old to be affected. The only action that can be taken is to remove the diseased leaves and burn them.

Leaf spot

Several different fungi may cause leaf spotting on camellias. One, *Pestalotiopsis*, may enter parts of a leaf that have been damaged by sunburn or in some other way. More common is another fungus, *Monochaeta camelliae*. The affected part usually becomes silvery grey and may have black, pinhead-size bodies of the fungus showing.

The first line of defence against leaf spotting is sound cultural practices to avoid leaf damage. Reducing the possibility of stress through injury and removing and burning diseased wood and leaves are important precautions.

Root rot

The fungi that cause root rot flourish in waterlogged soil, and camellias planted in heavy soil with poor drainage will be susceptible. There are several of these fungi, the main one being *Phytophthora cinnamomi*. The symptoms will probably not show until the weather is hot, when the leaves will become yellow and die, and the branches will wilt and die back from the tip until the plant itself is lost.

Camellias suffering from root rot may be stunted but survive for a considerable time in poor condition before finally dying. Examination of the root system will show that there are few, if any, of the white fibrous roots essential for a healthy plant. Roots of the affected plant will be dark brown and brittle.

Once again the importance of effective drainage and sound cultural practices must be emphasised. If the problem is identified soon enough, it may be possible to lift the plant and treat it before replanting it under better conditions in fresh soil. Treatment involves washing off all soil, cutting back any diseased roots to clean material, and soaking the roots in a fungicide solution for about twenty minutes. This treatment is impossible for large plants in the open ground and would be useless unless the drainage were to be improved. It is, however, a practicable procedure for container-grown or small camellias. Metalaxyl applied to the soil may be effective for treating large plants.

The fungi that cause root rot are present in many soils and may be introduced in the soil of a container-grown plant from a nursery. They are unlikely to affect healthy plants growing in well-drained and aerated soil.

Petal blight

Flower or petal blight, *Ciborinia camelliae*, previously classified as *Sclerotinia camelliae*, only affects plants of the genus *Camellia*. It is present in China, Japan and the United States but has not been reported in Europe, Australia or New Zealand.

The flowers are the only parts infected. From small tan or brown spots the disease spreads until the whole flower may become brown. Veins become darker so that infected flowers have a netted effect. It is this feature that distinguishes flower blight from climatic injury.

Many Americans are concerned about this disease, and because of its prevalence, some growers concentrate on container culture. Whether the camellias are grown in the ground or in containers, special precautions must be taken to control the blight and prevent its spread. The daily picking up and burning of all fallen petals is one such precaution.

The developing stages of petal blight, photographed in the United States.

'Crimson Robe', showing the typical yellow patches of virus on the leaves. The whole plant will be virus-affected.

New Zealand and other countries free from this curse must take every possible means to ensure that flower blight never becomes established. The main precaution is to follow implicitly regulations concerning the importation of plant material.

Virus diseases

Camellias can be infected by viruses that cause irregular blotches of white on coloured flowers and irregular blotches of yellow or pale colour on the foliage. In many instances, when this is not extensive, the plant does not appear to be harmed. The lack of chlorophyll, however, will prevent the proper functioning of leaves. The greater the virus-affected area, the greater the harm to the general health of the plant.

In France every effort is made to eliminate all viruses by destroying infected plants. In the United States, however, variegated flowers are so admired that some growers are quick to introduce a virus to solid-coloured cultivars by grafting onto infected stock.

'Ringspot' is another disorder in which a virus causes faint green rings to appear on leaves. On older leaves, these rings show as bright green spots with a darker edge, and the rest of the leaf turns yellow. The only action to be taken is to remove the leaves from the plant and destroy them.

There is no evidence, yet, that viruses are transferred to camellias by insects, though it is claimed in Britain that sap-sucking aphids and scale are guilty of doing so. Similarly, there is no evidence that they are spread by unclean secateurs or other tools, though every care must be taken to ensure that all tools are thoroughly clean and sharp. Viruses are definitely introduced by grafting onto affected stock, and by using scions from infected plants as cuttings. If a virus is present, the whole plant will be affected, and the virus-induced variegation will be likely to appear at some time.

Pests

There are a number of insect pests that may affect camellias. These may be classified generally in four groups. Some adversely affect plant health and strength by sucking the sap. A large number do little more than disfigure plants by chewing the leaves. There is another group that may tunnel into the stems. Members of the fourth group do not actually damage the plants but they can be a major nuisance.

While the broad groups of sucking, chewing, tunnelling and general-nuisance insect pests will be the same wherever one grows camellias, the particular culprits will vary from place to place. Insects that chew camellias in New Zealand, for example, may not be known in other countries.

Not all insects are pests; some are the camellia grower's friends and should be identified. Too often horticultural advisers and manufacturers of chemical poisons advocate the indiscriminate use of toxic sprays with no regard for those beneficial insects that aid the healthy development of camellias. Chemical poisons sprayed onto plants are not selective—they will kill the good as well as the bad.

Ladybirds (except those with 26 or 28 spots, which are leaf-eaters), praying mantises and many hover flies and lacewings should be encouraged in the garden. Ladybirds and their larvae feed on aphids, scales and mealybugs, as do praying mantises. Hover flies lay eggs near aphids, which provide food for their larvae when they hatch. Lacewings and their larvae also attack soft-bodied insects.

Even wasps can have their good points. Some, like the braconid wasp, are parasites of aphids and scales; others are predators. Early in the spring the dreaded European wasp, *Vespula germanica*, includes insects in its diet and attacks some pests. Two recent introductions to New Zealand, the Asian and Australian paper wasps, *Polistes chinensis* and *Polistes humilis*, annoying though they may be, attack caterpillars, and leaf rollers now seem to be less noticeable in some areas.

Some gardeners are not upset by a few chewed leaves and do nothing about pest control unless an infestation becomes particularly serious. To others, even one disfigured leaf is unacceptable. Gardeners must formulate their own programmes for pest control, but the first step is to identify the cause of any problem.

If you decide to spray, be sure to follow directions carefully and to take every precaution that is recommended when mixing and spraying chemical poisons. Wear rubber gloves and a good mask approved for chemical use, and remember that these sprays are dangerous if used carelessly.

The amount of spray required varies according to the pest to be controlled. Usually only the growing tips need to be sprayed to control aphids. Other pests are most frequently found on the undersides of leaves, so this should be the target area. A small aerosol can of an appropriate spray, obtainable from a garden centre, is likely to be all that a gardener needs.

It is possible to avoid spraying chemicals in the home garden. The award-winning bloom 'Wildfire' on page 8 was produced in a garden that had never experienced a pesticide spray. Investigations are being carried out to determine if it is possible to use poisons to eliminate pests without affecting insects that are beneficial. Most pests are leaf-eaters or suck sap from the leaves, whereas the friendly ones feed on the pests, not on plant material. Those growers who decide to apply insecticides by spraying should make enquiries about recent products that are safe to handle, are highly toxic to insects, remain on foliage longer and decompose rapidly in the soil.

A procedure that was developed in America has been tried by some growers with varying results. It is offered here for growers prepared to experiment, but please note carefully the warnings from the American experience. Not enough is yet known about the full effects of the process to recommend it unreservedly. It may be worthwhile for interested growers to try the practice in a restricted way and record their results. The process involves applying, with a cheap paint brush, a systemic insecticide, one that is absorbed into the plant, in a band about 4 cm (1.5 in.) wide around the lower trunk of the tree. The pests feeding on the foliage should be poisoned without any effect on the friendly ones, who will seek out their diet of aphids and scale insects elsewhere. This technique could be used in late spring, on cultivars that seem to attract most attention from pests. In severe cases it might be repeated about five months later.

The practice is used in South Carolina, in the United States, to control scale insects, but other sucking insects may also be controlled. Dr Luther W. Baxter, a plant pathologist, reports that a few *C. japonica* cultivars there have been found susceptible to either the material or the material applied this way. 'Wildwood' and 'Erin Farmer' were two cultivars affected seriously, but more than fifty others were not injured. Many trunks of camellias in the Maclay Gardens in Tallahassee, Florida, were painted, but apparently concern has led to the practice being discontinued. The American Camellia Society horticulturist, Betty Hotchkiss, reports that in the Massee Lane Camellia Gardens they do not risk damaging plants by painting the trunks.

Sucking insects

APHIDS

These pests may become a problem when the plant is growing strongly. Aphids are very small and are usually found on new shoots or buds, but they may feed on the undersides of older leaves. Shoots and leaves attacked by aphids may become twisted and wilt; buds may fail to open or may develop distorted flowers. Honeydew from aphids and from scale may result in a black coating on the leaves, called sooty mould.

Hosing will remove aphids, but if left, their numbers may be reduced by wasps, ladybirds, hover flies or lacewings. A systemic insecticide is an effective remedy. Soapy water may also be used, but this will only kill insects it touches and will not be effective for more than a day.

SCALE INSECTS

There are a number of different species of scale insect that can cause considerable damage to camellias if not controlled. They vary in shape, size and colour; some have hard shells, some soft. Ladybirds and parasitic wasps keep the numbers down, but in severe cases it may be desirable to prune and burn branches.

The best chemical control is obtained with all-purpose spraying oil; insecticides such as maldison or carbaryl may also be added. These are contact poisons of relatively low toxicity to humans but are highly toxic to bees and other beneficial insects.

THRIPS

These are not often a problem with camellias. If they do become established, it is likely that they started on some other host plant growing nearby. As one grower has said, 'They come to the camellias for dessert.' Leaves affected by

Aphids

Soft scale

Hard-backed scale

the rasping feeding action of thrips have a silvered appearance. Thrips have few insect enemies, and maldison is an effective insecticide.

Chewing insects

Each camellia-growing country has its own species of leaf-eating insects. Some, feeding at night, have probably never been identified. Others, like snails, grasshoppers and katydids, are well known for damaging a variety of plants and include camellias in their diet.

ADULT GRASS GRUB

The grass grub, *Costelytra zealandica*, is the most serious insect pest in New Zealand farm pastures and lawns. In summer, the shiny, golden-brown, hard-bodied adult beetles emerge and fly at dusk, and the adults feed voraciously on camellia leaves, among other things.

Pesticide granules spread over a lawn may reduce the number of grubs. Starlings are a natural enemy. One way of keeping the beetles from the foliage is to maintain a strong, steady spray of water when they are flying.

BAG OR CASE MOTH

The larvae of this moth, *Liothula omnivorous*, make bag-like structures for protection. It appears that these larvae may be responsible for much of the leaf chewing of camellias in some areas.

The most effective control is to remove the cases by hand and squeeze them firmly. However, there are likely to be many other cases high in other trees. When ready, the flightless female moths will lay eggs inside each case. The larvae will leave that shelter and disperse to make their own cases.

BRONZE BEETLE

The adult beetle, *Eucolaspis brunnea*, has similar habits to the adult grass grub, feeding on foliage in summer. Use control as for other chewing insects.

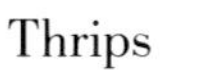
Thrips

Bag or case moth

Leaf-roller caterpillar

LEAF-ROLLER CATERPILLAR

The name comes from the caterpillar's habit of using silken threads to roll a leaf for a shelter. It will damage foliage and buds, and is most prevalent on the new spring growth of camellias. The caterpillars are difficult to reach with spray. Some predators attack them, and some birds feed on them extensively. A useful technique is to develop a keen eye for them and to squeeze the caterpillar in its shelter between thumb and forefinger.

Tunnellers

LEAF-MINERS

Larvae of several different insects feed inside the leaves of camellias. The unsightly 'mines' are easily seen, sometimes looking like thin, wavering lines and sometimes like blisters. A systemic insecticide should be an effective control.

STEM-BORERS

The grubs of several different beetles may damage camellias by burrowing in the wood. The first sign of the presence of borer may be sawdust pushed out from the burrows. The branch attacked will become unhealthy-looking and die back. At the first sign of fresh sawdust it may be possible to push a fine wire down the burrow to kill the grub, but this is rarely satisfactory. Syringing with weak insecticide or soapy water is always effective. Otherwise control is achieved by pruning and burning damaged branches.

General nuisances

ANTS

Though they do not themselves directly harm camellias, ants affect the plants through their eating habits. Honeydew, a sugary substance produced by aphids and scales, is left on the plant to become a popular food for ants. Predators of aphids and scales, such as ladybirds, avoid places where ants are moving about. Ants can be controlled with pesticide granules scattered at the base of the camellia.

CICADAS

Camellias are sometimes damaged by egg-laying females cutting into branches or the trunk of young plants to lay their eggs, usually in a 'herringbone' pattern. There is no chemical control. Eggs should be removed by pruning branches soon after they have been attacked.

CHAPTER 8

Propagation

Raising new varieties from seed

The camellia flower is bi-sexual, having both male and female reproductive organs, and is therefore capable of self-pollination. The male organ is the stamen, made up of the anther, which holds grains of pollen, carried on a stalk known as a filament. The female organ is the pistil, consisting of the stigma, which catches pollen at the top of the style, connected to the ovary. When pollination occurs, ripe pollen is transferred from a stamen to a stigma. When the stigma is receptive it secretes a sticky substance. Fertilisation occurs when the pollen grains reaching the stigma grow down the style to unite with the ovule in the ovary.

When the ovule has been fertilised, seeds develop in capsules or pods. Seed-pods ripen in the autumn and, if not collected beforehand, will split open to disperse the seed(s) around the base of the tree. After germinating, the new seedling may take from two to eight years to produce its first flowers, and it may be a further two or three years before the flowers are consistent in shape and form. The flowers of this new seedling may be very similar to, but will not be exactly the same as, the flowers of the parent plant. Only self-pollinated, wild species reproduce the same plant and flowers.

Where pollination by bees has occurred, the seed parent will be known if the seed is collected before it falls from the tree. However, the pollen donor, the male parent, will not be known. An educated assumption based on observation of leaf, flower and growth characteristics must be made for the new plant to be classified as belonging to a particular species. Thousands of excellent cultivars have come from growing these 'chance seedlings'. Some popular camellias whose full parentage is not recorded include 'Spring Festival', a *C. cuspidata* seedling; 'Tui Song', a seedling of *C. reticulata*

Opposite: A bee among the stamens of 'Prima Ballerina'. Many beautiful camellias come from chance seedlings that are the result of flowers being pollinated by bees and other insects.

'Cornelian'; and 'San Marino', another *C. reticulata* seedling.

Controlling pollination and raising new varieties from seed can be done systematically by studying genetics and chromosome counts, carefully selecting parents and keeping meticulous records. It is advisable first to set an objective for the hybridising project—fragrance or new colour, earlier flowering or some other sought-after characteristic. Find out from camellia journals and by talking with hybridisers about progress towards this objective. Note which plants set seed readily and work with them. Keep records that will make things easier in the future. These records can show, for instance, whether or not pollination is successful on a dull day or how high the temperature needs to be in a particular locality. Successful hybridising is all a matter of chance. The more crosses made, the more chance of creating a worthwhile new variety.

Controlled (hand) pollination

1. Select the parent plants with the characteristics desired.

2. Select a flower-bud on the female parent that is swollen and about ready to open. It is important to choose one before it has had a chance to be contaminated by other pollen. The two selected cultivars can be used as either male or female parents.

3. Emasculate the flower. This is to eliminate the possibility of self-pollination and to allow the reproductive parts of the flower to be easily reached. The stigma will not yet be ready to receive the pollen, so a paper, not plastic, bag must be secured over the emasculated flower immediately to prevent contamination by other pollen. Hold the bud firmly and, with a sharp razor blade or small scissors, cut deeply enough around the entire flower, just above the green calyx, to remove the petals. With tweezers or small scissors, remove all the stamens, being careful not to damage the pistil and its stigma.

4. When the stigma of the emasculated flower is receptive, it will be sticky. Place pollen from the selected male parent on the stigma liberally. This can be done in various ways. The whole flower can be removed from the donor male parent and the pollen dusted on; a few pollen-carrying stamens can be removed and taken to the female parent and gently wiped onto the stigma; a small paintbrush, a matchstick or a fingertip can be used to carry pollen from one flower to the other. The donor parent flower should be bagged before it opens, to prevent any other pollen being deposited on it by wind, birds or insects.

5. The pollinated flower must be bagged immediately to prevent any other pollen reaching the stigma. The bag can be removed after about ten days, when fertilisation will be completed.

6. Label the pollinated flower with brief information about the parents and

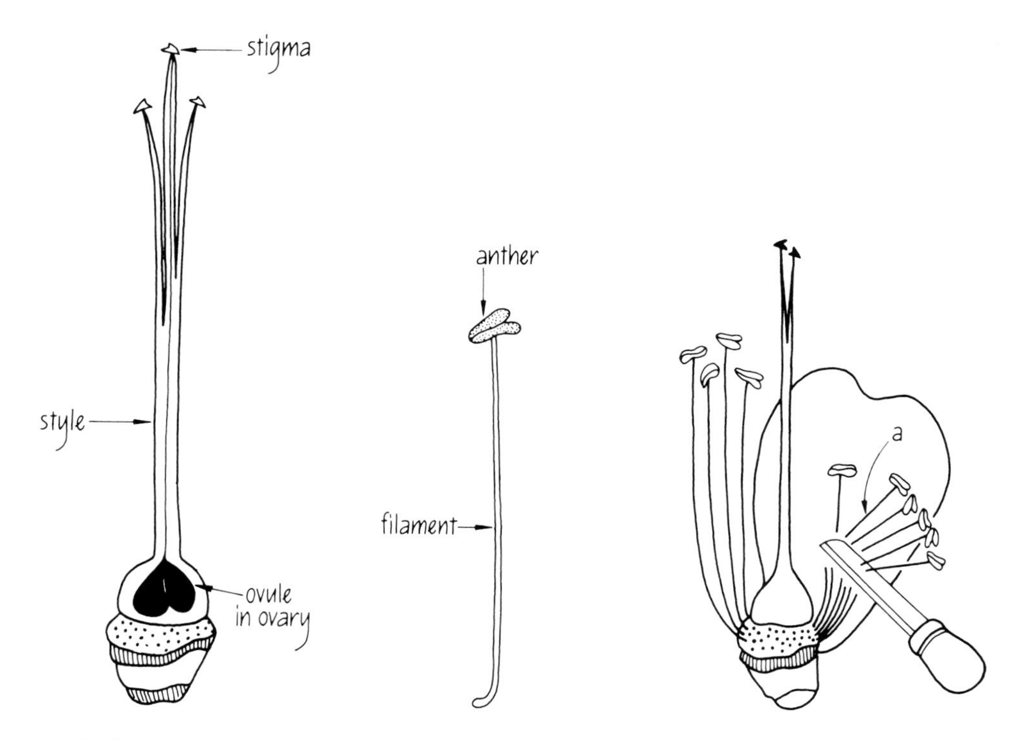

Left: Female reproductive organ, the pistil. Centre: Male reproductive organ, the stamen. Right: Emasculating a flower — all stamens are removed carefully to avoid self-pollination.

the date of the cross. Add as much other detail as needed to help with any planned programme of hybridisation.

Raising seedlings

The seed-pod will have begun to swell soon after fertilisation and will continue to grow bigger until it ripens in the autumn. Harvest the seed-pod when it is starting to split, just before it has matured fully, cracked open and ejected the seeds. If several crosses have been made, ensure that the seeds are correctly identified. Break the pods open and germinate the seed as soon as possible.

Warmth, moisture and darkness are the requirements for germination. Seeds can be placed on 3–4 cm (1.2–1.5 in.) of well-dampened, but not wet, sphagnum moss, or even tissue paper, in an accurately labelled jar that is sealed with a screw top, or some other means to retain the moisture. Place seeds around the inside of the jar on this moss. Cover them with another layer of sphagnum, then more seeds, and continue until the jar is topped up with sphagnum. The jar can then be stored in a warm, dark place like a hot-water cupboard. Germination is likely to begin in about two weeks but may take much longer if the seed is not very fresh. While waiting for germination, check the jar regularly to ensure that the sphagnum moss has not dried out.

Alternatively, soil or some other medium such as perlite, vermiculite, or a mixture of sand and peat can be placed in a flat tray. Seeds should be planted about 1 cm (0.5 in.) deep with the 'eye', where the root will emerge, facing down. After placing the seed in position, water thoroughly with a fine spray or mist and allow to drain. The soil medium should not be allowed to dry out during the germination period. Place the tray in a warm, sheltered place. If it is deep enough, it may be covered with a sheet of glass or plastic, or enclosed in a plastic bag. Bottom heat from a correctly wired bench in a greenhouse can speed up the germination process.

A slower procedure is to plant the seeds in a clearly marked corner of the garden.

For seeds germinated in a jar, germination can be seen as the white radicle or tap-root develops against the side of the jar and grows quickly downwards. When this radicle is about 3 cm (1.2 in.) long, the seed should be carefully removed from the jar. This task can be made easier by using tweezers to remove the sphagnum from the centre of the jar, leaving space to ease the seeds out without damage.

It is the usual practice to nip off the tip of the radicle at this stage to promote the formation of side roots. This restriction of the tap-root will make the seedling easier to handle as it is moved progressively from pot to pot.

The seedling should now be planted in a small pot or in a tray in light, porous, water-retentive potting mix. A commercial potting mix or something like a mixture of peat and pumice will be suitable. Plant the rooted seedling with the seed case sitting on top of the potting mix, which should be pressed firmly around the root. Seeds germinated in a tray or in the garden will be ready to plant out in individual pots when two or three leaves appear. Seedlings planted in trays should be moved to pots before the roots become entangled.

Great care must now be taken. The seedling has just been removed from

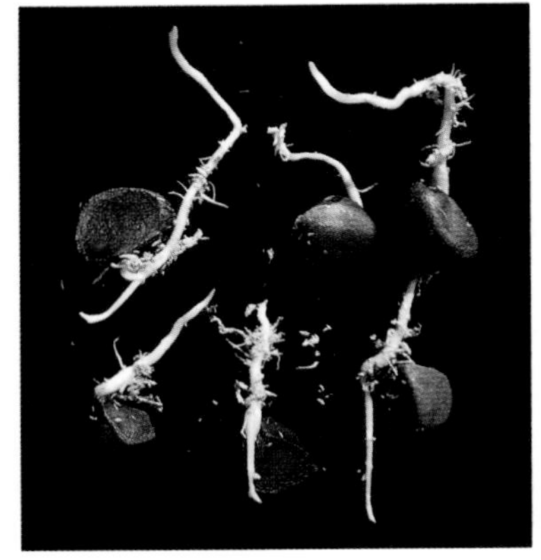

Left: Seed-capsules split open to release seeds. Centre: Germinated seeds ready for planting. Right: Seeds planted on top of the potting mix with the shortened taproot firmly in place.

The rapid annual growth of young camellias is clearly shown by these one-, two- and three-year-old seedlings.

the completely sheltered environment of the jar, which also provided ideal warmth and moisture. A warm, sheltered position out of the direct sun is essential. Keep the seedling in a greenhouse or inside the house, or sit the pot in a plastic bag, allowing the sides to sit up above the developing plant, shielding it from draughts. Adequate light and air are the two other ingredients now required.

As the young plant grows and the roots fill the pot, it should be moved to a slightly larger pot. This can be a yearly procedure, each time leaving about 5 cm (2 in.) between the roots and the outside of the pot for further growth, until the plant is ready for its permanent home in a container or the open ground. If the potting mix does not contain fertiliser, a feeding programme should be started. This could be a weekly spraying with a weak solution of fish emulsion or liquid blood and bone.

If a new camellia seems to be something special, experienced growers should be asked to evaluate it and compare it with ones already in circulation. While the new camellia is likely to be an attractive garden plant, unless it has some special qualities not present in others it will not justify naming and registration. The national camellia society is responsible for registration. Information can be obtained from the nearest branch or from the national organisation.

Reproducing known varieties

While growing plants from seed creates new varieties, raising plants from cuttings or by layering or grafting will produce camellias exactly the same as the plant from which the cutting or grafting material was obtained. However, there are two exceptions to this. First, if a sport—a flower that differs from the named variety it is found on—is discovered, it can be propagated using one of these procedures and named as a new plant. Second, if the understock is virus-infected, the grafted plant will also be infected.

A grower with a greenhouse and aids such as bottom heating and overhead misting will know how to adapt what is suggested here and make the best use of all resources. These notes are primarily for growers who do not have these facilities.

Cuttings

The best time to take cuttings is when the new growth is hardening. These half-hardy cuttings are the most successful for establishing roots. This will generally be in the summer, but with some varieties there will be another phase in late autumn. However, do not refuse the offer of cuttings at other times. With care, they may establish successfully.

The cutting should be from the latest growth, brown in colour, and about 8 cm (3.5 in.) long with several leaves. Cut off the lower leaves, keeping two or three at the top, and trim these back by about half to reduce the loss of water. The cutting must have at least one strong leaf-bud at the top. It is also possible to take leaf cuttings—just a leaf and a node with a small heel of the stem attached. The process will be the same as for wood cuttings, except they are not planted as deeply.

If a cutting cannot be planted immediately, it may be sealed in an airtight plastic bag that has been dampened inside. It can be kept for some time in this bag in a refrigerator. A simple way to label the cutting is to place it on a hard surface, then, using a ballpoint pen, print its name firmly on the leaf. The name will be engraved indelibly.

The rooting medium should lack nutrients so that the developing roots are encouraged to search widely for them. Sand or pumice with some peat is effective. Untreated sawdust, perlite or vermiculite are other possibilities. The container for the rooting mix will depend upon the number of cuttings to be set out. A depth of at least 10 cm (4 in.) for the mix and at least 8 cm (3.5 in.) of headroom for the leaves should be allowed. Place 10 cm (4 in.) of the mix in the container, water it well and allow it to drain.

Prepare the cuttings by making a long, tapering cut at the base of the stem. This leaves plenty of the cambium layer exposed on which a callus will form before roots emerge. Trim off the extremely thin tip of the stem. Dampen the cut end and dip it in a rooting-hormone powder, shaking off any excess. The hormone powder should speed up the rooting process.

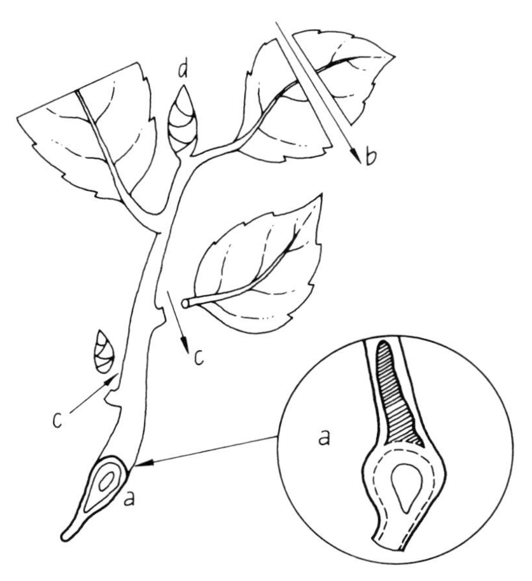

Preparation of cuttings: (a) The base is prepared with a long, tapering cut with some bark removed (inset) to increase the cambium area for callusing and root development. (b) The upper leaves are shortened to reduce the loss of moisture. (c) The lower leaves and buds are removed. A strong vegetative leaf-bud (d) remains, from which new growth will appear.

Make holes in the planting mix at regular intervals, 5–8 cm (2–3.5 in.) deep, with a large nail or pencil. These should be wide enough apart to keep the cuttings separated and preferably on an angle. Plant one cutting to each hole, being careful not to rub off the hormone powder. Firm the mix around the cuttings.

After planting, cuttings need to be kept damp in a reasonably warm, protected place, out of direct sunlight. If they are in a tray, a sheet of glass, plastic or newspaper across the top will help retain moisture and protect the cuttings. If they are in a pot, an inverted glass jar can be used. Alternatively, two U-shaped wires can be pushed into the mix and a polythene bag pulled over and tied. Each of these types of cover will help to maintain essential humidity.

Cuttings from different cultivars will take different lengths of time to callus and root. Reticulatas are notoriously difficult to grow from cuttings and are usually propagated by grafting. Roots will begin growing on some cuttings in about six or seven weeks. Some can be checked after this time and, if the roots are 5 cm (2 in.) or more long, the cutting can be planted in its own pot.

The first pot should be small, allowing about 5 cm (2 in.) of space around the roots. Normal potting mix can now be used and a fertilising programme started. In these early stages a weekly spraying with a very weak solution of fish emulsion or liquid blood and bone will suffice. Care should be taken in hardening off the new plant, and the soil should be kept moist. The cutting should be moved to a larger pot before it becomes rootbound, again allowing about 5 cm (2 in.) of space around the roots.

Air layering

This method is based on a process developed by the Chinese centuries ago. Air layering is a technique with a high success rate because the part to be

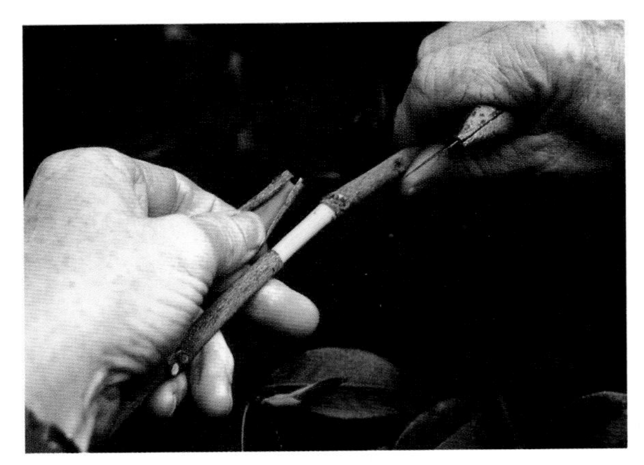

Step 1: A ring of bark and the cambium layer are stripped from the branch.

Step 2: Damp sphagnum moss has been placed over the prepared section and, step 3, wrapped carefully with polythene.

Step 4: After about six months, strong-growing roots are intermingled with the sphagnum.

Air layering

rooted is still attached to the plant. It is a simple procedure resulting in many relatively large plants exactly the same as the parent plant, ready in about six or seven months. All that is needed are a sharp knife, sphagnum moss, black polythene or aluminium foil cut in rectangles approximately 10 cm (4 in.) square, and strong string or waxed thread. Air layering can be carried out with camellias when the new growth has hardened in late spring or early summer.

1. Select a healthy, vigorous, well-shaped branch. Make the layer about 30 cm (12 in.) from the tip, or up to 60 cm (24 in.) to give a bigger plant. With a sharp knife, make two parallel cuts around the branch, about 5 cm (2 in.) apart. Remove the ring of bark between these two cuts and scrape away the cambium layer, the green tissue between bark and wood.

2. Thoroughly wet a handful of sphagnum moss, then squeeze out all excess water so that it is not soggy. Completely cover the prepared section of the

branch with the sphagnum. Some people dust the branch with rooting-hormone powder before covering it but this is not essential.

3. Wrap a polythene or aluminium foil square snugly around the moss and tie it securely at each end. It should be tight enough to prevent evaporation and the entry of rain. A few small holes pricked on the underside of the cover will allow any surplus water that accumulates to drain away. Too much moisture would damage newly forming roots.

4. The layer can be left unattended for about six months. As the roots develop they will fill up the space with the sphagnum moss inside the wrapping. When the layer is hard to press it will be full of roots. Cut off the rooted branch from the parent plant just below the air layer. Remove the wrapping but do not disturb the entanglement of moss and roots. Cut off the stump as close to the roots as possible without damaging them. Remove about half the foliage to keep it in balance with the roots.

5. Plant the camellia using the methods described on page 79. Do not plant it too deeply, and give it extra water and shade. If it is to be planted in the open ground, choose the position carefully. Otherwise plant it in a container, at least until the root system has fully developed.

Grafting

Grafting is a process of encouraging material from one plant (the scion) to grow on the root system of another plant (the understock). If a camellia fails to produce sufficient attractive flowers in spite of being healthy, a desirable variety may be grafted onto its established root system. Some camellias, such as reticulatas, do not grow readily from cuttings, and grafting is the best way to propagate them. Grafted plants, because of the strong root system, will grow quickly in the first few years until the foliage is in balance with the root system.

There are many different methods of grafting. It is generally accepted, however, that cleft grafting is the most dependable, and this is the method used by nurseries, but it can be fun for a hobbyist to try other ways. Whether cleft grafting, side grafting, approach grafting, whip grafting or cutting grafting, the key to success is to have contact between cambium layers to effect a union through callusing.

Most grafting will be onto an understock growing in a container. The same techniques can be adapted for use on mature trees growing in the open ground. The understock to be used should be selected carefully. Vigorous-growing plants will be best. Research has shown that sasanqua varieties, particularly 'Kanjiro', have the advantage of being resistant to root rot. Reticulata hybrids are also worth using. While japonica varieties may be used as understock for their own kind, do not graft a fast-growing reticulata cultivar onto a slower-growing japonica understock, as this will result in an unsightly and weak development known as 'bottlenecking'. Avoid using as understock a plant that is still adjusting to the shock of recent repotting or transplanting.

It has often been said that the time to graft is when a desirable and healthy scion, with about four leaf nodes, is obtained. Grafting will probably be successful at most times of the year, except during the period of actual growth. In fact, the best time is about six to eight weeks before new growth begins. This allows adequate time for the union to callus before the buds burst into leaf.

The tools required for grafting should be assembled before starting: a very sharp knife, lopping shears, perhaps a small saw with fine teeth, a small screwdriver, material to tie the graft (rubber bands, grafting tape, sticking plaster, raffia or plastic tape can all be used), a large jar or plastic bag, and two long, U-shaped wires. A plastic jar with a screw top and the bottom cut out makes an excellent cover. When it is time to allow some air into the graft, the screw top can be removed easily.

Attention to plant hygiene is always important. It is a good idea to soak scions in a fungicide and to wipe the grafted areas with the fungicide as well. Tools, of course, should be clean as well as sharp.

Do not give up if you do not have a 100 per cent success rate from the beginning. You may lose some grafts for various reasons but, if you observe carefully what is happening, you will soon develop a satisfactory technique and will rarely lose any. Label each graft carefully, including the date and the name of the scion and the understock, so that you begin to learn which plants give most success.

CLEFT GRAFT

1. With the lopping shears or a small saw, cut off the stock on a slight angle a few centimetres above the soil level. Trim the cut surface smooth with a sharp knife and bevel the sides of the stump so that moisture drains away.

2. Again using a sharp knife, split the stump down to a sufficient depth, about 5 cm (2 in.), to take the scion. There is a danger in this operation of the knife slipping, so holding the stump firmly with a pair of pliers is a sensible precaution.

3. Prepare the scion by trimming the end of the stem to a wedge shape about 3–5 cm (1.5–2 in.) long, with one side a little thicker than the other.

4. Using the screwdriver, force open the slit in the understock. Insert the scion carefully with the thicker edge of the wedge to the outside. It is crucial that there is as much contact as possible between the cambium layers of scion and stock so they will knit together and grow. If the wedge was prepared properly, it should be possible to feel whether the scion is correctly placed. The scion may be tilted very slightly outwards to ensure that the cambium layers are in contact in at least two places.

5. In most cases there will be enough pressure to hold the graft when the screwdriver is pulled from the stock. To be sure, however, it is wise to tie it firmly. Grafting paste may be spread over the joined areas, although this is not essential.

6. The graft should now be covered and made airtight. If a jar is used, this can be achieved simply by piling some sand around its base. Keep the covered graft in a sheltered place, protected from the sun but in the light. If a camellia growing in the ground has been used as understock, it will be necessary to shield the cover on the sunny side.

7. Inspect the graft regularly, occasionally allowing air in for a short time before making it airtight again. If the scion has lost one leaf, the graft may still be successful. However, if all leaves drop off, this effort has failed. If there is still time before new growth is anticipated, it is possible to start again by cutting the stock off a little lower than before.

If the understock bleeds, fungus may develop. Keep mopping up the moisture and, if there are signs of fungus, wipe the area with a fungicide solution.

8. When the union between understock and scion has taken and the scion begins to shoot, the plant should be hardened off. This operation must be carried out carefully and with patience. The edge of the cover should be lifted or the screw top removed to allow air to circulate around the graft for a short while. Watch carefully, allowing a little longer exposure to air each day, but

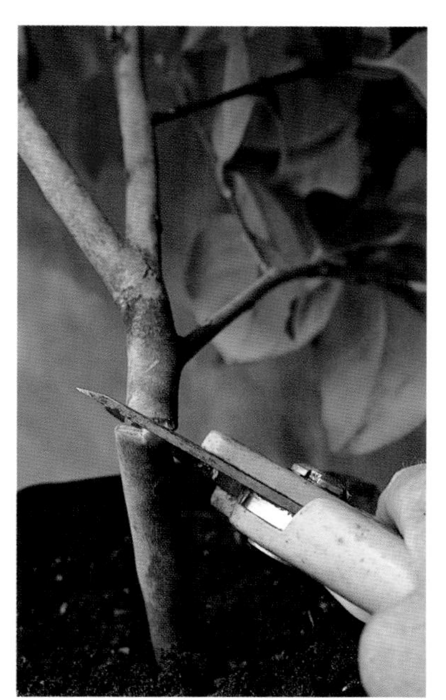

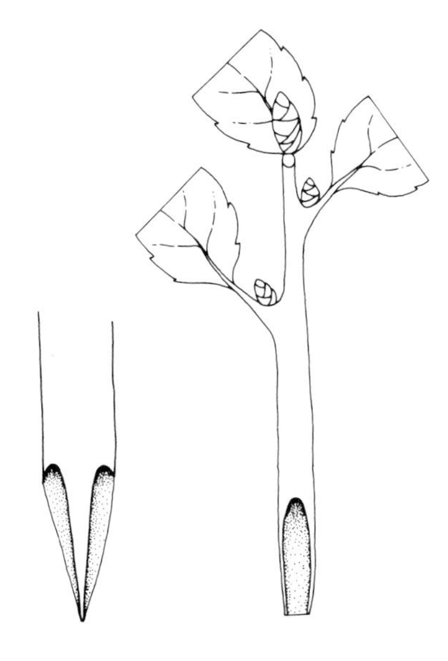

Cleft grafting. Left: The top of a young plant is removed on an angle to leave the understock. Centre: The stock is slit ready to receive the scion. Right: The scion is prepared like a cutting, with its base cut in a wedge shape.

Cleft grafting. Left: The scion is fitted into the understock with the green cambium layers touching. Centre: Wires are fitted in a planter bag to keep the covering clear of the trimmed leaves. Right: The covering is in place and made airtight.

if there are any signs of wilting, make the cover airtight again until the graft recovers. If the cover is removed completely too soon, the new graft will collapse.

SIDE GRAFT

A side graft can be made with smaller stock and may allow for more contact between the cambium layers.

1. Cut the stock down but leave a few leaves still growing.

2. Make a slanting cut about 2.5 cm (1 in.) long into the side of the stock with a very sharp knife.

3. Prepare the scion as for a cleft graft but make one cut side longer than the other, as illustrated. This will allow for a better match between scion and cut in the stock.

4. Set the scion in place in the stock, making sure that there is as much cambium contact as possible.

5. Follow the procedures for covering and care set out earlier until the graft has united well and begun to grow.

6. When the graft has knitted strongly and there is healthy new growth, the stock above the graft can be removed completely.

SADDLE GRAFT

This involves a further variation in the preparation of the scion and the understock. After the understock is reduced to a stump, cut the top of it in the shape of a sharply tapered wedge. Split the scion up the centre and place it as a 'saddle' over the tapered wedge of the understock. If the scion is a similar size to the understock, this should ensure a large degree of cambium contact, and excess sap from the understock is unlikely to cause any trouble.

Standard camellias can be created using cleft-, saddle- or side-grafting techniques. Any variety can be grafted onto a suitable understock such as 'Kanjiro', and those with a weeping growth habit are especially attractive. The understock should be a single stem, though some other branches and leaves should be left on the plant until the graft is growing. It may be any height up to about 2 metres (6 feet).

It is important to maintain constant humidity around the graft until it knits. This is achieved by packing some damp sphagnum moss around the cover—a bottle, jar or plastic bag around a wire frame—and tightly sealing it. A 1.25 litre (2 pint) plastic soft-drink bottle is an ideal cover. Remove the coloured

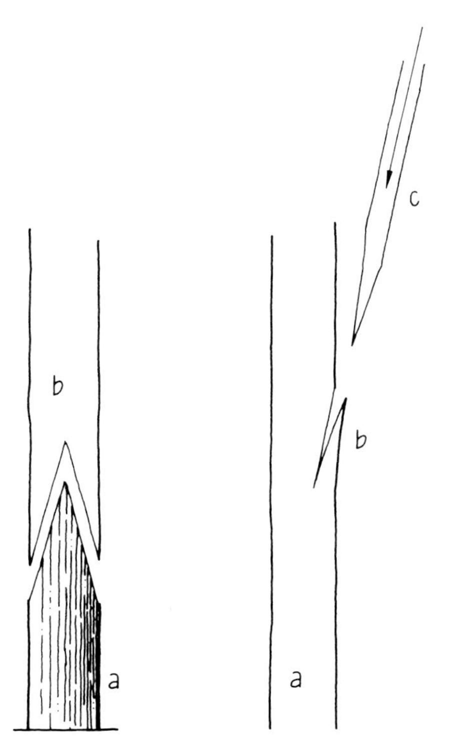

Alternatives to the cleft graft. Left: Saddle graft, in which the scion (b) fits neatly over the understock (a). Right: Side graft, in which the scion (c) is joined to the understock (a) in an angled cut (b).

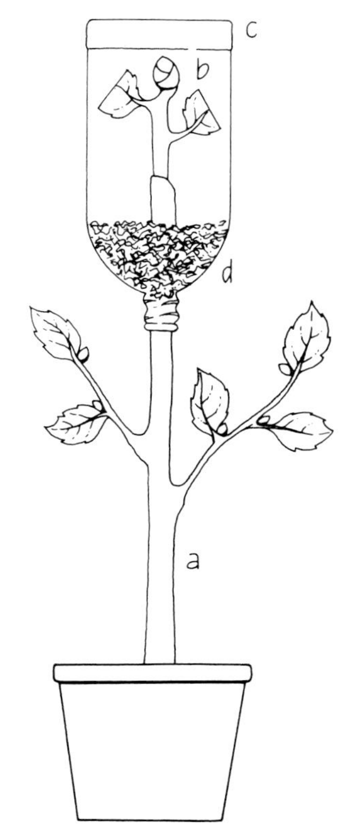

Grafting a standard. The scion (b) is united to a suitable understock (a) by a cleft graft. The graft is protected by an inverted bottle (c), inside which is damp sphagnum moss (d).

'cup' and cut out the base of the bottle, then invert it and slide it down over the stem of the stock plant until the graft is made. The bottle can then be fixed in position and the cup replaced. The graft should be supported with stakes and kept cool and shaded.

CUTTING GRAFT

The cutting graft method brings together the techniques of side grafting and propagation from cuttings. It is used with camellias that do not grow well on their own roots or to provide a root system that is more resistant to root rot.

1. For the understock, remove a strong top shoot from a sasanqua variety such as 'Kanjiro' and prepare it as for a cutting. It will help if this shoot is similar in thickness to the scion to be used.

2. Make a sloping cut 1.5 cm (0.5 in.) long into the stem about 5 cm (2 in.) up from the bottom. Be careful not to cut right through the stem.

3. Prepare a scion approximately 8 cm (3.5 in.) in length with two leaves at the top. Cut the base into a wedge shape about 1.5 cm (0.5 in.) long.

4. Insert the scion in the cut made in the understock, aligning the cambium layers on one side at least. Tie them together or keep them firm with a rubber band.

5. Treat the graft as any other cutting but plant it deeply enough to cover the union by about 2.5 cm (1 in.).

6. When roots have developed from the base of the cutting understock and the union has callused, the new plant is ready for potting. At this stage cut off the unwanted top of the understock above the union but as close to the union as possible and remove any roots that have formed at or above the union.

NURSE SEED GRAFT

This technique is simple, requires minimal equipment and eliminates the bending and crouching that is part of most other grafting.

Seeds that have germinated and sent up about 5 cm (2 in.) of new growth are selected as nurse stock. At this stage the stems will be green and the leaves will not yet have unfolded. A very young plant such as this is supported by the seed cotyledons through short petioles or leaf stalks until it is able to survive alone.

1. Select a good-sized seed. Cut it from the seedling through the petioles. If this is done without damage to the roots, the seedling will carry on to form a plant.

2. Holding the seed carefully against a firm base, push the point of a knife gently between the petioles into the seed cotyledons to make an opening for the scion.

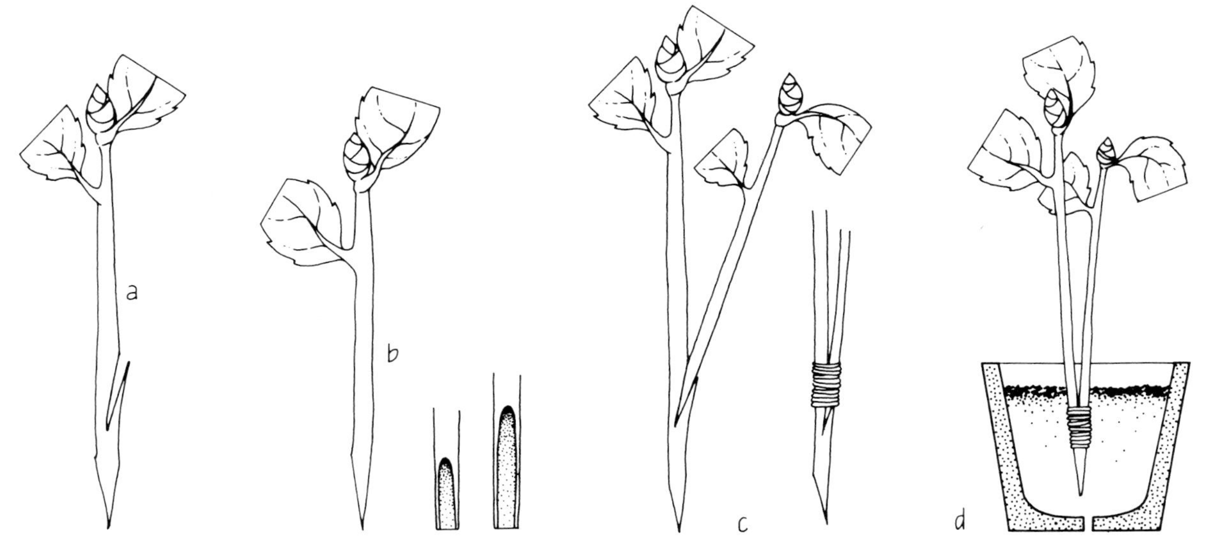

Cutting graft. (a) The cutting selected as understock has a slit in the side to receive the scion. (b) The scion is prepared in a wedge shape, with one side cut longer than the other. (c) The scion is fitted into the understock and tied securely. (d) The cutting graft is planted, with the union just below the surface of the potting mix.

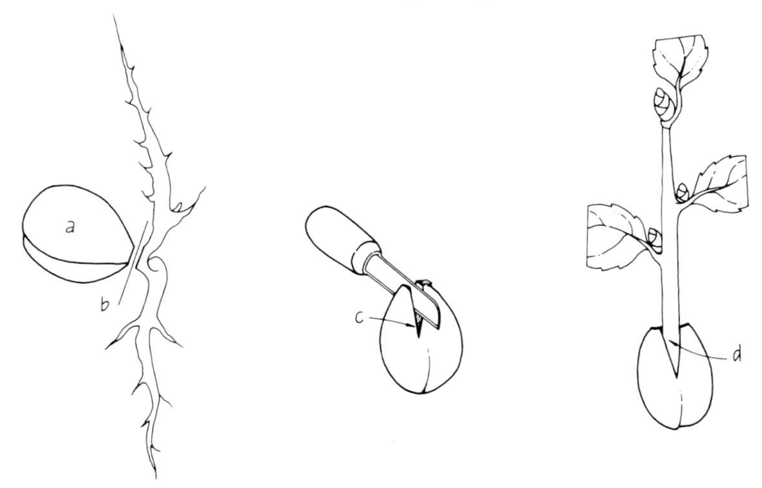

Nurse seed graft. (a) A germinated seed selected for the graft. (b) The young developing plant is cut from the seed. (c) A slit is cut in the seed to receive the scion. (d) The scion in position, ready for planting.

3. Trim the scion to a wedge shape and press it firmly into the opening made for it.

4. Plant the graft in a mix suitable for cuttings with the union about 3 cm (1.5 in.) below the surface. Now care for the graft in the same way as cuttings. The cambium of the scion will unite with the cambium of the cotyledon petioles, through which it will draw food from the cotyledons during this early stage.

APPENDIX 1

Annotated list of camellia species and cultivars

The descriptions of the 400-odd camellias in this list include the country of origin and the year of registration (or some other significant year marking availability of the cultivar); the colour, size and form of the flowers; the growth habit of the plant; and the flowering season (VE = very early, E = early, M = midseason, L = late, VL = very late). Some descriptive information has been derived, with permission, from *Camellia Nomenclature* and Camellia Haven (NZ) catalogues.

Species camellias

C. chekiangoleosa: China; red, medium to large, single, funnel-shaped flowers; semi-shade recommended when young.

C. chrysantha: also known as *C. nitidissima;* China; yellow, small, single to semi-double flowers; large, quilted, leathery leaves, bronze coloured when young, new growth several times a year; sensitive to heat and cold; fast, upright growth; M–L.

C. cuspidata: China; white flowers with widely flared stamens; pointed, narrow leaves; tall growth; M.

C. forrestii: China, SE Asia; white, very small, fragrant flowers; leaves pointed both ends; M.

C. fraterna: China; white, small, fragrant flowers; leaves pointed with serrations; tall growth; M.

C. granthamiana: Hong Kong; white, very large flowers; large, leathery leaves; small, spreading tree; E.

C. grijsii: China; white, small, single flowers; small, shiny, quilted leaves; medium, bushy growth; M–L.

C. kissi: China, Nepal, NE India, Burma, SE Asia; white, small, single flowers, often fragrant; variable leaves; may grow to tall tree; M–L.

C. longicarpa: China; white, very small, single, cup-shaped flowers; vigorous, spreading growth; M–L.

C. lutchuensis: islands south of Japan; white, tiny, very fragrant flowers; very small leaves from green to bronze; difficult to grow; M–L.

C. lutchuensis Formosan Form: much lower, denser growth than the usual *C. lutchuensis*; M–L.

C. oleifera (also known as *C. drupifera*): China, Hong Kong, SE Asia, Burma, NE India, Thailand; white, small, single flowers with long, twisted petals; slow, dense, sturdy growth; M–L.

C. pitardii: China; white flushed with pink, small, single flowers; slow growth; M–L.

C. rosiflora: China; pink, miniature, cupped, single flowers; strong, upright, bushy growth; M.

C. salicifolia: Hong Kong, Taiwan; white, single flowers with slight fragrance; slender, willow-like leaves, opening pink through bronze to green; weeping habit; M–L.

C. saluenensis: China; flowers variable from white to rose-pink; compact growth; M–L.

C. sinensis: China, Tibet, Taiwan, Japan, Thailand, Burma; white, miniature flowers; long, narrow, crinkled leaves; strong, bushy growth, but variations according to variety; the commercial tea plant; VE.

C. transnokoensis: Taiwan; white, miniature, fragrant flowers opening from ornamental pink buds; dense, upright growth; M–L.

C. tsaii: China, Burma, SE Asia; white, miniature flowers; wavy, elongated leaves on arching branches; M.

C. vietnamensis: Vietnam; white flowers, sweetly scented; small tree, vigorous, bushy growth; E–M.

C. yunnanensis: China; white, small flowers with a wide burst of stamens; fast, upright growth with coarse-textured leaves; summer display of rosy red seed-pods like small apples; M–L.

Japonica cultivars

'Ace of Hearts': USA, 1963; deep red, medium to large, semi-double; vigorous, compact, upright growth; M.

'Adolphe Audusson': France, 1877; dark red, large, semi-double; medium, compact growth; M.

'Ai-no-izumi': soft pink, small, formal double; dense, compact growth; L.

'Akashi-gata': Japan, 1887; priority name for 'Lady Clare'; deep pink, large, semi-double; vigorous, bushy growth; E–M.

'Akebono': Japan, 1930; light pink, medium, semi-double of cupped form; compact growth; M.

'Alba Plena': China, 1792; white, medium, formal double; slow, bushy growth; E.

'Alice Wood': USA, 1960; bright red, large, formal double; vigorous, upright growth; E–M.

'Alison Leigh Woodroof': USA, 1955; pale pink shading to glowing pink at edge, small, semi-double; vigorous, compact, upright growth; M.

'Allie Habel': USA, 1965; shell-pink edged deeper pink, medium to large, peony form; medium, compact growth; M.

'Amazing Graces': USA, 1979; blush-pink shading to deeper pink at edge, small, formal double with swirled inner petals; medium, open, upright growth; M.

'Ann Sothern': USA, 1960; venetian-pink shading to porcelain-white in centre, large, semi-double with upright petals among white stamens; vigorous, compact, upright growth; E–M.

'Annie Wylam': USA, 1959; bright pink shading to white in centre, medium, peony form with many slender petaloids; medium, open, upright growth; E–L.

'Antarctic Star': NZ, 1981; white, medium, anemone form; medium growth; M–L.

'Aquarius': USA, 1971; medium pink, medium, formal double; slow, compact, upright growth; M–L.

'Arajishi': Japan, 1891; dark salmon-rose, medium, full peony form; vigorous, open, upright growth; E.

'Aspasia Macarthur' or 'Aspasia': Aust., 1850; white to cream-white with a few rose-red lines and dashes, medium, full peony form; slow, upright growth; E–M.

'Augusto L'Gouveia Pinto': Portugal, 1890; light coral-pink sometimes flushed with lavender and each petal bordered white, large; slow, open growth; E–M.

'Ave Maria': USA, 1956; silvery pink, small to medium, formal double; slow, compact, upright growth; E–M.

'Ballet Dancer': USA, 1960; cream shading to coral-pink at edge, medium, full peony form with mixed petals and petaloids of full form; medium, compact, upright growth; E–L.

'Bambino': USA, 1959; coral-rose-pink, small, peony to anemone form; vigorous, bushy, upright growth; M.

'Bea Rogers': USA, 1971; alabaster-white, large, peony form; medium, upright growth.

'Berenice Boddy': USA, 1946; light pink with deep pink under petals, medium, semi-double; vigorous, upright growth; M.

'Betty's Beauty': USA, 1975; sport of 'Betty Sheffield Supreme'; white with red picotee edge, large, informal double; average, upright growth; M.

'Black Tie': USA, 1968; dark red, small, formal double; very strong, upright growth; M–L.

'Blaze of Glory': USA, 1965; brilliant red, large, anemone form; medium, compact, upright growth; E–M.

'Blood of China': USA, 1928; deep salmon-red, medium, semi-double to loose peony form; vigorous, compact growth; L.

'Bob Hope': USA, 1972; very dark red, large, semi-double; very glossy foliage, average, upright growth; M–L.

'Bob's Tinsie': USA, 1962; brilliant red, miniature to small, anemone form; medium, compact, upright growth; M.

'Bokuhan': Japan to USA, 1930; priority name for 'Tinsie'; red outer guard petals and white peony centre, miniature, anemone form; vigorous, upright growth; E–M.

'Bonbon': USA, 1961; white splotched red, miniature, peony form; vigorous, upright growth.

'Botan-yuki': *C. japonica* subsp. *rusticana*; very pale blush-pink with yellow petaloids, miniature, anemone form; dense, compact growth; L.

'Brushfield's Yellow': Aust., 1968; white with cream to yellow petaloids, medium, anemone form; dense, compact, upright growth; M–L.

'Burgundy Boy': NZ, 1985; very dark red, small to medium, semi-double; slow, compact growth; M–L.

'C. M. Hovey': USA, 1853; dark red, medium, formal double; medium, slender, upright growth; L.

'C. M. Wilson': USA, 1949; sport of 'Elegans'; light pink, large to very large, anemone form; slow, spreading growth; E–M.

'Can Can': Aust., 1961; sport of 'Lady Loch'; pale pink with darker pink veining and petal edges, medium; E–M.

'Cara Mia': USA, 1960; pink shading to blush-pink in centre petals, medium to large, semi-double; vigorous, upright growth; E–M.

'Cardinal's Cap': USA, 1961; cardinal-red, small, anemone form; medium, compact, upright growth; M–L.

'Carter's Sunburst': USA, 1959; pale pink striped or marked deeper pink, large, semi-double to peony form to formal double; medium, compact growth; E–L.

'Charlie Bettes': USA, 1960; white with deep yellow stamens, large to very large, semi-double; vigorous, compact growth; E.

'China Doll': USA, 1958; blush-white edged coral, medium to large, loose high-centred peony form with fluted petals; medium, compact growth; M.

'Chinese Lanterns': USA, 1972; blush-pink, miniature, rose-form double; medium, open growth; M.

'Cho Cho San': Japan to USA, 1936; light pink, medium, semi-double to anemone form; medium, compact growth; M.

'Commander Mulroy': USA, 1961; white edged pink with pink bud centre, medium, formal double; medium, compact, upright growth; M.

'Coquettii': also known as 'Glen 40'; USA, 1942; deep red, medium to large, formal double; slow, compact, upright growth; M–L.

'Coronation': USA, 1954; white, very large, semi-double; vigorous, open, spreading growth; M.

'Cottontail': white, miniature, full peony form; medium, compact, upright growth; M.

'Cover Girl': USA, 1965; clear pink, medium to large, formal double with irregular petals; strong, upright growth; M–L.

'Crane's Feather': NZ, 1967; white, very large, anemone form; slow, open growth; M.

'Cream Puff': USA, 1986; chalky white, medium, peony form; medium, compact growth; M.

'Crimson Glory': USA, 1959; crimson, medium, semi-double with petaloids and red stamens; slow, open growth; M–L.

'Dahlohnega': USA, 1986; canary-yellow, small to medium, formal double; slow, open, upright growth; M.

'Debutante': USA, early 1900s; light pink, medium, full peony form; vigorous, upright growth; E–M.

'Demi-Tasse': USA, 1962; peach-blossom pink, small to medium, semi-double of hose-in-hose form; vigorous, compact, upright growth; M.

'Desire': USA, 1977; pale pink edged deep pink, medium, formal double; vigorous, compact, upright growth; M.

'Dixie Knight': USA, 1955; deep red, medium, loose peony form with irregular petals; vigorous, upright growth; M–L.

'Dolly Dyer': Aust., 1973; scarlet, miniature, anemone form; vigorous, upright growth; E–M.

'Donna Herzilia de Freitas Magalhaes': Portugal, 1952; red with distinct violet shade, medium, semi-double to anemone form; M.

'Dorothy Culver': USA, 1978; white, large, peony form; vigorous, upright growth; M.

'Dr Lilyan Hanchey': USA, 1976; very pale blush-pink, medium, formal double; medium, open, upright growth; M.

'Dr Tinsley': USA, 1949; very pale pink at base shading to deeper pink at edge with reverse side flesh-pink, medium, semi-double; compact, upright growth; M.

'Drama Girl': USA, 1950; deep salmon-rose-pink, very large, semi-double; vigorous, open growth; M.

'Easter Morn': USA, 1965; baby pink, very large, semi-double with irregular petals to full peony form; medium, upright growth; M–L.

'Ecclefield': USA, 1959; white, large to very large, semi-double to anemone form; vigorous, compact, upright growth; M.

'Elegans': England, 1831; rose-pink with centre petaloids often spotted white, large to very large, anemone form; slow, spreading growth; E–M.

'Elegans Champagne': USA, 1975; sport of 'Elegans Splendor'; white with cream centre petaloids; same form and growth habit.

'Elegans Splendor': USA, 1969; sport of 'C. M. Wilson'; light pink edged white with deep petal serrations.

'Elegans Supreme': USA, 1960; sport of 'Elegans'; rose-pink with very deep petal serrations.

'Elizabeth Weaver': USA, 1975; coral-pink, large, formal double; medium, open, upright growth; E–M.

'Elsie Ruth Marshall': USA 1965; light pink to purplish pink, large, rose-form double; vigorous, upright growth; M–L.

'Erin Farmer': USA, 1962; white washed and shaded orchid-pink, large, semi-double to loose peony form with twisted, curled petals; vigorous, upright growth; M.

'Fashionata': USA, 1964; apricot-pink, large, semi-double with curled outer petals; vigorous, open, upright growth; M.

'Fimbriata': China to England, 1816; sport of 'Alba Plena' with fringed petals, medium; M.

'Fircone': USA, 1950; blood-red, miniature, semi-double; vigorous, bushy growth; M.

'Fire Falls': USA, 1955; glowing crimson, medium to large, full peony form; vigorous, open, upright growth; E–L.

'Fran Homeyer': USA, 1974; pearl-pink, large, formal double; medium, spreading growth, E–M.

'Gayle Walden': USA, 1954; light pink, medium, peony to anemone form; vigorous, upright growth; M.

'Ginger': USA, 1958; ivory-white, miniature, full peony form; medium, upright growth; M–L.

'Golden Temple': Japan, 1941; known as 'Daitairin'; light rose-pink, large, single mass of petaloids in centre; vigorous, upright growth; E.

'Grace Albritton': USA, 1970; light pink deeper at edge, miniature to small, formal double; medium, upright growth; M.

'Grand Prix': brilliant red, very large, semi-double with irregular petals; vigorous, upright growth; M.

'Grand Slam': USA, 1962; brilliant dark red, large to very large, semi-double to anemone form; vigorous, open, upright growth; M.

'Grand Sultan': Belgium, 1849; dark red, large, semi-double to formal double; slow, open growth; M–L.

'Great Eastern': Aust., 1873; rose-red, medium to large, semi-double with irregular petals; vigorous, bushy growth; M.

'Guest of Honor': USA, 1955; salmon-pink, large to very large, semi-double to anemone to peony form; vigorous, upright growth; M.

'Guest Star': USA, 1974; pink shading to white, medium, formal double; medium, compact growth; M–L.

'Guilio Nuccio': USA, 1956; coral-rose-pink, large to very large, semi-double with irregular petals; vigorous, upright growth; M.

'Gwenneth Morey': Aust., 1965; white outer petals and deep cream to pale primrose-yellow petaloids, medium, anemone form; medium, upright growth; usually indistinguishable from 'Brushfield's Yellow'; M–L.

'Hagoromo': Japan, 1886; also known as 'Magnoliiflora'; blush-pink, medium, semi-double; medium, compact growth; M.

'Hakuhan-kujaku': Japan, 1956; known as the peacock camellia; red mottled white, small, single, slender, tubular petals; medium, semi-cascading growth; M–L.

'Harry Cave': NZ, 1991; deep scarlet-red, medium, semi-double; slow, compact growth; E–M.

'Hawaii': USA, 1961; sport of 'C. M. Wilson'; pale pink, medium to large, peony form with fimbriated petals; slow, spreading growth; E–M.

'Helen Boehm': USA, 1977; blush-pink, large, peony to anemone form; medium, upright growth; M.

'Henry Turnbull': Aust., 1950; white, large, semi-double; spreading growth; E.

'Himatsuri': *C. japonica* subsp. *rusticana*; rose-red blotched white, miniature, loose anemone form.

'Holly Bright': USA, 1985; glossy salmon-red, large, semi-double with creped petals; medium, compact, upright growth; unique crinkled, holly-like foliage; M.

'In The Purple': NZ, 1982; dark to purplish red with darker veining, medium, peony form; average growth; M–L.

'Janet Waterhouse': Aust., 1952; white, large, semi-double; M.

'Jean Clere': NZ, 1969; sport of 'Aspasia Macarthur'; red with narrow band of white around edge, medium.

'Jury's Yellow': NZ; white with cream to yellow petaloids, medium, anemone form; similar to 'Brushfield's Yellow' and 'Gwenneth Morey'; strong, upright growth; M–L.

'Just Sue': Aust., 1971; sport of 'Margaret Davis'; light pink edged red, medium, informal double; strong, upright growth, M–L.

'K. Sawada': USA, 1940; white, large, formal to rose-form double; vigorous growth; M.

'Kathryn Funari': USA, 1975; deep veined pink, large, formal double; medium growth; E.

'Katie': USA, 1979; salmon-rose-pink, very large, semi-double; vigorous, upright growth; E–M.

'Kewpie Doll': USA, 1971; chalky light pink, miniature, anemone form; vigorous, bushy, upright growth; M.

'Kick Off': USA, 1962; pale pink marked deep pink, large to very large, loose peony form; vigorous, upright growth; E–M.

'Kingyo-tsubaki': also known as 'Quercifolia'; strawberry ice cream to scarlet coloured, large, single; fishtail leaves; E–M.

'Kitty Berry': USA, 1956; light peach-pink, medium, loose peony form; medium, compact, upright growth; M.

'Kramer's Supreme': USA, 1957; turkey-red, large to very large, full peony form, fragrant; vigorous, compact, upright growth; M.

'Kumagai' (Nagoya): dark red with flared white stamens capped with pink and white petaloids, large, single; Higo form.

'Kuro-tsubaki': Japan, 1896; black-red with red stamens, small, semi-double; medium, compact growth; M–L.

'Lady Loch': Aust., 1898; sport of 'Aspasia Macarthur'; light pink sometimes veined deeper pink and edged white, medium; strong, upright growth; M–L.

'Lady Vansittart': Japan to England, 1887; white striped rose-pink, medium, semi-double with broad, wavy-edged petals; slow, bushy growth; M–L.

'Laurie Bray': Aust., 1955; soft pink, medium to large, semi-double with spaced and ruffled petals; upright growth; M.

'Lemon Drop': USA, 1981; white with lemon centre, miniature, rose-form double to anemone form; medium, upright growth; M.

'Leonora Novick': USA, 1968; white, large to very large, loose peony form; medium, upright growth; E–M.

'Lily Pons': USA, 1955; white, medium, single to semi-double with very long, narrow petals surrounding a cluster of long stamens; medium growth; M.

'Little Babe': USA, 1974; dark red, small, rose-form double; vigorous, compact growth; E–L.

'Little Ginger': USA, 1977; pink at edge fading to white in centre, small, formal double; medium, upright growth; L.

'Little Slam': USA, 1969; rich red, miniature, full peony form; medium, upright growth; E–M.

'Lovelight': USA, 1960; white, large, semi-double with heavy petals; vigorous, upright growth; M.

'Lucy Hester': USA, 1959; silver-pink, large to very large, semi-double of lotus form; vigorous, upright growth; M.

'Madame Picouline': Belgium, 1855; also known as 'Akaroa Rouge'; cherry-red, medium, informal double; average, upright growth; VE–M.

'Man Size': USA, 1961; white, miniature, anemone form; medium, open growth; M.

'Margaret Davis': Aust., 1961; sport of 'Aspasia Macarthur'; white to cream-white with a few rose-red lines and edged bright vermilion, medium, informal double; strong, upright growth; M–L.

'Margarete Hertrich': USA, 1944; white, medium, formal double; vigorous, compact, upright growth; M.

'Mark Alan': USA, 1958; wine-red, large, semi-double to loose peony form with long narrow petals and petaloids; strong, upright growth with long flowering season; E–M.

'Maroon and Gold': USA, 1961; maroon, small to medium, loose peony form with golden stamens; vigorous, upright growth; M–L.

'Mary Agnes Patin': USA, 1961; china-rose, large, rose-form double with some upright, fimbriated petals and occasional cluster of petaloids; vigorous, open, upright growth; E.

'Melissa': USA, 1961; blush-pink, miniature, semi-double.

'Mermaid': often incorrectly called 'Kingyo-tsubaki' because of fishtail leaves; rose-pink, medium, semi-double to rose-form double; vigorous, spreading growth; M.

'Midnight': USA, 1963; black-red, medium, semi-double to anemone form; vigorous, compact, upright growth; M.

'Misty Morn': NZ, 1982; pale pink at edge fading to white at base, medium, formal double; medium growth; M–L.

'Modern Art': NZ, 1973; red heavily variegated with stripes and spots of other shades of red, large, semi-double; M.

'Moonlight Bay': USA, 1982; light orchid-pink, very large, semi-double; vigorous, compact, upright growth; E–L.

'Mrs D. W. Davis': USA, 1954; blush-pink, very large, semi-double; vigorous, upright growth; M.

'Mrs D. W. Davis Descanso': USA, 1970; sport of 'Mrs D. W. Davis'; full peony form.

'Moshio': Japan to Aust.; deep red, medium, semi-double; upright compact growth; M.

'Nuccio's Gem': USA, 1970; white, medium to large, formal double; vigorous, compact, upright growth; E–M.

'Nuccio's Jewel': USA, 1977; white washed and shaded orchid-pink, medium, full peony form; slow, bushy growth; M.

'Nuccio's Pearl': USA, 1977; white washed and shaded orchid-pink, medium, formal double; vigorous, upright growth; M.

'Onetia Holland': USA, 1954; white, large to very large, loose peony form; medium, compact growth; M–L.

'Otome': Japan to USA, 1975; also known as 'Pink Perfection'; pink, small, formal double; vigorous, upright growth; E–L.

'Pink Pagoda': USA, 1963; rose-pink, medium to large, formal double; vigorous, compact, upright growth; M.

'Pink Smoke': USA, 1965; light lavender-pink, miniature, loose anemone form; fast, bushy growth; E–M.

'Pirates Gold': USA, 1969; dark red, large, semi-double to loose peony form; medium, spreading growth; M–L.

'Polar Bear': Aust., 1957; chalk-white, large, semi-double.

'Powder Puff': USA, 1960; white, small to medium, peony form; medium growth; M.

'Premier': USA, 1965; clear rose-red, large, full peony form; vigorous, upright growth; M–L.

'Pride of California': USA, 1977; orange-pink, miniature, formal double; slow growth; M.

'Prima Ballerina': USA, 1983; white washed and shaded orchid-pink, medium to large, semi-double with fluted petals; medium, compact growth; M–L.

'Queen Diana': NZ, 1985; pink shading to pale pink in outer petals, medium, formal double; vigorous, open growth; E–L.

'R. L. Wheeler': USA, 1949; rose-pink, very large, semi-double to anemone form with heavy outer petals and solid circle of stamens; vigorous, upright growth; E–M.

'Raspberry Ice': USA, 1987; light rose-pink with white petal edges and streaks of raspberry on each petal; average, upright growth; M.

'Red, Red Rose': USA, 1969; bright red, medium to large, formal double with high centre like a rose; vigorous, bushy, upright growth.

'Reigyoku': Japan to USA, 1975; orange-red, small, single; compact growth, glossy green foliage with blotch of pink in centre of each leaf when young turning to light yellow on maturity; M.

'Roger Hall': Aust., 1979; clear red, medium, formal double; vigorous, upright growth; E–L.

'Royal Velvet': USA, 1987; dark velvet-red, large, semi-double; vigorous, upright growth; M.

'Rudolph': USA, 1981; deep red, medium, full peony form; medium, upright growth; E–M.

'Ruffian': USA, 1978; white with yellowish tinge,

large, semi-double with irregular petals to peony form; medium, upright growth; M–L.

'San Dimas': USA, 1971; dark red, medium to large, semi-double with irregular petals; medium, compact growth; E–M.

'Sanpei-tsubaki': pink with darker veining and white border, small, single; strong, upright growth; M.

'Scentsation': USA, 1967; silvery pink, medium to large, peony form, fragrant; medium, compact, upright growth; M.

'Shiro Chan': USA, 1953; sport of 'C. M. Wilson'; white with light basal pink when first opening, large to very large.

'Shiro-otome': Japan, 1907; white, medium, formal double; M.

'Silver Anniversary': USA, 1960; white, large, semi-double with irregular petals intermixed with golden stamens; vigorous, compact, upright growth; E–M.

'Silver Chalice': USA, 1963; white, medium to large, full peony form; vigorous, compact, upright growth; M.

'Silver Cloud': USA, 1980; white, very large, loose peony form; vigorous, upright growth; M–L.

'Silver Waves': USA, 1969; white, large to very large, semi-double with wavy petals; vigorous, bushy, upright growth; E–M.

'Snowman': USA, 1964; white, large, semi-double with curled petals; vigorous, spreading, upright growth; M.

'Something Beautiful': USA, 1983; pale pink edged burgundy-red, miniature, formal double; vigorous, compact, upright growth; M.

'Sugar Babe': USA, 1959; dark pink to red, miniature, formal double; slow growth; M.

'Sunset Glory': USA, 1951; coral-pink, large, anemone form with long guard petals; vigorous, open, upright growth; E–L.

'Swan Lake': USA, 1971; white, large, rose-form double to loose peony form; vigorous, compact, upright growth; M.

'Takanini': NZ, 1989; glowing dark red, medium, anemone form; strong, bushy growth with an exceptionally long flowering season; VE–VL.

'Tama-no-ura': Japan, 1973; red with white border, small, single; fast, spreading growth; E–M.

'The Elf': USA, 1984; light pink, medium, semi-double; slow, dwarf growth; M.

'Tiffany': USA, 1962; soft pink, very large, loose peony form, produces many undamaged flowers for picking; strong, bushy growth; M–L.

'Tinker Bell': USA, 1958; white striped pink and rose-red, small, anemone form; vigorous, upright growth; E–M.

'Toki-no-hagasane': Japan, 1934; white blushed pink with deeper pink under petals, medium, semi-double; slow, compact growth; L.

'Tom Knudsen': USA, 1965; dark red with darker veining, medium to large, formal to rose-form double to full peony form; vigorous, upright growth; E–M.

'Tom Thumb': USA, 1957; medium pink with each petal edged white, small to medium, formal double; medium, upright growth; M.

'Tomorrow Park Hill': USA, 1964; sport of 'Tomorrow'; variegated, light soft pink generally deepening towards edge; vigorous, open growth; E–M.

'Twilight': USA, 1964; palest blush-pink, large, formal double with many layers of petals; strong, upright growth; M–L.

'Un-ryu': Japan, 1967; deep pink, small, single; medium, upright growth, unusual zig-zag growth pattern; M.

'Ville de Nantes'; France, 1910; sport of 'Donckelaeri'; dark red blotched white, medium to large, semi-double with upright, fimbriated petals; M–L.

'Wilamina': USA, 1951; clear soft pink with darker pink edge, small, formal double with incurved petals; medium, compact growth; M.

'Wildfire': USA, 1963; orange-red, medium, semi-double; vigorous, upright growth; E–M.

'Yamoto-nishiki': Japan; white striped pink, medium, single.

'Yours Truly': USA, 1949; sport of 'Lady Vansittart'; pink streaked deep pink and bordered white, medium, semi-double; slow, bushy growth; M–L.

'Yukimiguruma': Japan; commonly known, incorrectly, as 'Amabilis'; white, medium, single; average, upright growth, good for floral work; M.

'Yuri-tsubaki': carmine-rose, 'hose-in-hose' blooms with long, lily-shaped petals; E–M.

Reticulata cultivars and hybrids with reticulata parentage

Note: Cultivars marked * do not have the large flowers and leaves typical of *C. reticulata.*

'Al Gunn': USA; rich medium pink, very large, semi-double with curled, incurved petals; vigorous, spreading, upright growth; M.

'Applause': USA, 1980; *C. reticulata* 'Mudancha' x *C. reticulata* 'Elizabeth Johnstone'; salmon-pink, large, loose peony form; vigorous, upright growth; M.

'Arcadia': USA, 1979; *C. reticulata* hybrid 'Mouchang' x *C. sasanqua* 'Bonanza'; salmon-pink, very large, semi-double to loose peony form; vigorous, open, upright growth; M–L.

'Arch of Triumph': USA, 1970; 'Wild Form' seedling; deep pink to wine-red, very large, loose peony form; vigorous, bushy, upright growth; E–M.

'Aztec': USA, 1971; *C. reticulata* 'Crimson Robe' x *C.*

japonica 'Lotus'; deep rose-red, very large, semi-double with loose petals to loose peony form; spreading, open growth; E–M.

'Barbara Clark'*: NZ, 1958; *C. saluenensis* x *C. reticulata* 'Captain Rawes'; cyclamen to rose-pink, semi-double, medium; strong, upright growth, E–L.

'Betty Ridley'*: USA, 1973; *C. japonica* 'Marie Bracey' x *C. reticulata* hybrid 'Felice Harris'; pink, large, formal double; slow, open, upright growth; E–M.

'Black Lace'*: USA, 1968; *C.* x *williamsii* 'Donation' x *C. reticulata* 'Crimson Robe'; dark red, medium to large, formal double; M–L.

'Brian'*: NZ, 1958: *C. saluenensis* x *C. reticulata* 'Captain Rawes'; rose-pink, medium, semi-double; strong, upright growth; M–L.

'Butterfly Wings': China to USA, 1948; also known as 'Houye-diechi'; a Yunnan *C. reticulata*; rose-pink, very large, semi-double with irregular, broad, wavy petals; slender, open growth; M.

'Camelot': Aust., 1976; rose-pink, large, semi-double; vigorous, open, upright growth; M.

'Cameron Cooper': USA, 1976; *C. reticulata* 'Cornelian' x *C. japonica* 'Mrs D. W. Davis'; vivid pink, very large, rose-form double to peony form; vigorous, compact, upright growth; E–L.

'Captain Rawes': China to England, 1820; parentage unknown; carmine-rose-pink, very large, semi-double with irregular petals; medium, open growth; L.

'Chrysanthemum Petal': China to USA, 1948; also known as 'Juban'; a Yunnan *C. reticulata*, light carmine-pink, medium, rose-form to formal double with fluted petals; slender, open growth; E.

'Cornelian': China to USA, 1948; also known as 'Damanao'; a Yunnan *C. reticulata*; turkey-red to deep rose-pink marbled white, large to very large, semi-double to peony form with irregular, wavy, crinkled, spiral petals and a few petaloids in the centre; vigorous, compact growth; M.

'Crimson Robe': China to USA, 1948; also known as 'Dataohong'; a Yunnan *C. reticulata*; carmine-red, very large, semi-double with wavy, crinkled, crepe-textured petals; vigorous, spreading growth; M.

'Curtain Call': USA, 1979; deep coral-rose, very large, semi-double with irregular petals; vigorous, open growth; M–L.

'Debut': USA, 1977; purplish red, very large, loose peony form; vigorous, compact, upright growth; M.

'Descanso Mist': USA, 1970; *C. reticulata* x *C. japonica*; red with iridescent petals, large, formal double to peony form; medium, upright growth; M.

'Dr Clifford Parks': USA, 1971; *C. reticulata* 'Crimson Robe' x *C. japonica* 'Kramer's Supreme'; red with orange cast, very large, semi-double, loose or full peony form or anemone form; vigorous growth; M.

'Dr Emil Carroll': USA, 1983; *C. reticulata* 'Crimson Robe' x *C. reticulata* hybrid; burgundy-red, very large, anemone form to loose peony form; medium, upright growth; M–L.

'Dream Girl': USA, 1965; *C. sasanqua* 'Narumi-gata x *C. reticulata* 'Buddha'; salmon-pink, large to very large, semi-double with fluted upright petals; vigorous, upright growth; E.

'Edith Mazzei': USA, 1982; *C. reticulata* 'Crimson Robe' x *C. reticulata* hybrid 'Jean Pursel'; rose-pink with deeper pink veining, large to very large, rose-form double to semi-double; medium, open, upright growth; M–L.

'Emma Gaeta': USA, 1979; *C. reticulata* 'Cornelian' x *C. reticulata* hybrid 'Mouchang'; deep rose-pink, very large, semi-double; vigorous, upright growth; M.

'Fire Chief': USA, 1963; *C. japonica* 'Donckelaeri' x *C. reticulata* 'Cornelian'; deep red, large, semi-double to peony form; medium, spreading, upright growth; L.

'Flower Girl': USA, 1965; *C. sasanqua* 'Narumi-gata' x *C. reticulata* 'Lionhead'; pink, large to very large, semi-double to peony form; vigorous, upright growth; E.

'Fluted Orchid'*: USA, 1960; *C. saluenensis* x *C. reticulata* 'Crimson Robe'; pale orchid-pink, medium, semi-double with fluted petals.

'Four Winds': USA, 1971; *C. reticulata* 'Crimson Robe' x *C. japonica* 'Tiffany'; orchid-pink, large to very large, semi-double; M.

'Francie L.': USA, 1964; *C. saluenensis* 'Apple Blossom' x *C. reticulata* 'Buddha'; rose-pink, very large, semi-double with irregular, wavy petals; M.

'Glowing Embers': NZ, 1976; *C. reticulata* 'Crimson Robe' x *C. reticulata* 'Lionhead'; red, very large, semi-double to loose peony form; medium, open, upright growth; E.

'Gwen Washbourne': NZ, 1974; *C. reticulata* seedling; reddish pink, very large, semi-double to loose peony form; medium growth; M.

'Harold L. Paige': USA, 1972; *C. japonica* 'Adolphe Audusson' x *C. reticulata* 'Crimson Robe'; bright red, very large, rose-form double to peony form; vigorous, spreading growth; L.

'Jean Pursel': USA, 1975; *C. reticulata* 'Crimson Robe' x *C. reticulata* hybrid; light purplish pink, very large, peony form; vigorous, upright growth; M–L.

'Jingan-cha': China to USA, 1980; a Yunnan *C. reticulata*; scarlet, very large, loose peony form; L.

'K. O. Hester': USA, 1972; orchid-pink, large to very large, semi-double with irregular, upright petals; vigorous, open, upright growth; M.

'Lasca Beauty': USA, 1973; *C. reticulata* 'Cornelian'

x *C. japonica* 'Mrs D. W. Davis'; soft pink, very large, semi-double with heavy-textured, thick petals; vigorous, open, upright growth; M.

'Lila Naff': USA, 1967; 'Butterfly Wings' seedling; silver-pink, large, semi-double with wide petals; vigorous, compact, upright growth, M.

'Lisa Gael': NZ, 1967; 'Purple Gown' seedling; rose pink, large, rose-form double; compact, upright growth; M.

'Lois Shinault': USA, 1973; *C. reticulata* 'Crimson Robe' x *C. granthamiana*; medium orchid-pink shading, lighter in centre, very large, semi-double with irregular petals ruffled on edges and upright centre petals; medium, spreading growth; E–M.

'Lovely Lady': Aust., 1981; seedling of *C. reticulata* hybrid 'Pink Sparkle'; soft pink with salmon cast, large, formal double with ruffled petals; compact, upright growth; M.

'Mandalay Queen': USA, 1966; 'Tali Queen' seedling; rose-pink, very large, semi-double with fluted petals; vigorous, open, upright growth; M–L.

'Margaret Hilford': NZ, 1980; parentage unknown; deep red, very large, semi-double; vigorous, open, upright growth; E–M.

'Miss Tulare': USA, 1975; 'Crimson Robe' seedling; bright red to rose-red, large to very large, rose-form double to full peony form; vigorous, upright growth; E–M.

'Mudancha': China to USA, 1948; a Yunnan *C. reticulata*; bright pink veined white and striped white on inner petals, large to very large, formal double with wavy, crinkled, crepe-like petals; medium growth; L.

'Nuccio's Ruby': USA, 1974; very dark rich red, large to very large, semi-double with irregular ruffled petals; medium, compact, upright growth; M.

'Otto Hopfer': USA, 1970; *C. reticulata* 'Crimson Robe' x *C. japonica* 'Lotus'; light red, large to very large, semi-double with irregular petals; vigorous, upright growth; M.

'Pavlova': Aust., 1978; clear bright red, very large, semi-double; vigorous, spreading, upright growth; M–L.

'Phyl Doak': NZ, 1958; rose bengal, large to very large, semi-double; compact, upright growth; E–L.

'Purple Gown': China to USA, 1948; also known as 'Shizetou'; a Yunnan *C. reticulata*; purple-red with white to wine-red pinstripes, large to very large, formal double to peony form with wavy petals; compact growth; M.

'Robert Fortune': China to England, 1857; also known as 'Pagoda'; a Yunnan *C. reticulata*; deep scarlet, large, deep formal to rose-form double; compact growth; M.

'Royalty': USA, 1968; *C. japonica* 'Clarise Carleton' x *C. reticulata* 'Cornelian'; bright pink, deeper in centre, very large, semi-double with wavy, crinkled petals; medium, upright growth; M.

'Ruby Queen': NZ, 1984; *C. reticulata* 'Crimson Robe' x *C. reticulata* 'Purple Gown'; vibrant red, very large, semi-double; vigorous, upright growth; M.

'S. P. Dunn': USA, 1981; *C. reticulata* 'Crimson Robe' x *C. reticulata* hybrid; red, very large, semi-double; vigorous, upright growth; M–L.

'Samantha': Aust., 1967; 'Cornelian' seedling; china pink, very large, semi-double to loose peony form.

'San Marino': USA, 1975; *C. reticulata* seedling; dark red, large, semi-double with heavily textured petals; medium, spreading, upright growth; M.

'Sandy Clark': NZ, 1970; *C. reticulata* 'Buddha' x *C. saluenensis*; soft pink, large semi-double; vigorous, upright growth; M.

'Satan's Robe': USA, 1965; *C.* hybrid 'Satan's Satin' x *C. reticulata* 'Crimson Robe'; oriental-red, large, semi-double; vigorous, upright growth; M.

'Shot Silk': China to USA, 1948; also known as 'Dayinhong'; a Yunnan *C. reticulata*; brilliant spinel-pink, large, semi-double with loose, wavy petals; vigorous growth; E.

'Show Girl': USA, 1965; *C. sasanqua* 'Narumi-gata' x *C. reticulata* 'Lion Head'; pink, large to very large, semi-double to peony form; vigorous, open, upright growth; E–M.

'Sugar Dream'*: NZ, 1984; *C. reticulata* hybrid 'Dreamgirl' x *C. oleifera* 'Jaune'; medium pink, medium, anemone form; medium, open, upright growth; E.

'Tali Queen': China to USA, 1948; also known as 'Dali-cha'; a Yunnan *C. reticulata*; turkey-red to deep pink, very large, semi-double with irregular petals; medium, upright growth; M.

'Terrell Weaver': USA, 1974; *C. reticulata* 'Crimson Robe' x *C. japonica* 'Ville de Nantes'; flame to dark red, large, semi-double to loose peony form with thick, fluted and twisted petals; vigorous, spreading, upright growth; M.

'Tui Song': NZ, 1967; 'Cornelian' seedling; rose-pink, large, semi-double; upright growth; M.

'Valentine Day': USA, 1969; *C. reticulata* 'Crimson Robe' x *C. japonica* 'Tiffany'; medium salmon-pink, large to very large, formal double with rosebud centre; vigorous, upright growth; M.

'Valley Knudsen': USA, 1958; *C. saluenensis* x *C. reticulata* 'Buddha'; deep orchid-pink, large to very large, semi-double to loose peony form; vigorous, compact, upright growth; M–L.

'Warwick Berg': NZ, 1978; *C. saluenensis* x *C. reticulata* 'Crimson Robe'; clear bright red, very large, formal double; upright growth; M.

'William Hertrich': USA, 1962; *C. reticulata* 'Cornelian' seedling; deep cherry-red, very large, semi-double with large, somewhat reflexed outer petals and smaller, loosely arranged, upright inner petals with some folded and intermixed with stamens; vigorous, bushy growth; M.

'Willow Wand': China to USA, 1948; also known as 'Liuye-yinhong'; a Yunnan *C. reticulata*; light orchid-pink, large, rose-form double to semi-double with irregular, wavy petals; vigorous, upright growth; M.

'Woodford Harrison': USA, 1980; *C. reticulata* 'Crimson Robe' x *C. reticulata* hybrid; deep rose-red, veined, very large, semi-double; vigorous, spreading, upright growth; M–L.

Sasanqua and heimalis cultivars, and hybrids with sasanqua parentage

Note: Unless stated otherwise, each cultivar in this section is early-flowering and of spreading growth.

Hiemalis cultivars:

'Bonsai Baby': deep red, small, formal to rose-form double; low, spreading growth.

'Chansonette': brilliant pink, large, formal double with ruffled petals.

'Dazzler': rose-red, large, semi-double.

'Elfin Rose': rose-pink, azalea-form double.

'Interlude': light pink, large, rose-form to formal double.

'Kanjiro' (often called 'Hiryu'): rose-pink shading to rose-red on edges of petals, large, semi-double; tall and bushy.

'Peerless': bright rose-pink, medium, loose peony form.

'Shishi-gashira': red, medium, semi-double to double.

'Showa Supreme': soft pink, large, peony form.

'Showa-no-sakae': soft pink, medium, semi-double to rose-form double.

Sasanqua cultivars and hybrids with sasanqua parentage:

'Beatrice Emily': violet-red with white petaloid centre, medium, anemone form.

'Bert Jones': silver-pink, medium, semi-double; long flowering season.

'Bettie Patricia': soft pink, formal double; slow growing.

'Bonanza': deep red, large, semi-peony form; long flowering season.

'Choji-guruma': light pink turning deeper towards edge of petals and petaloids, medium, anemone form.

'Early Pearly': white with blush centre petals, small, rose-form double.

'Exquisite': pale pink, large, single.

'Fukuzutsumi': also known as 'Apple Blossom'; white shaded rose-pink, large, single to semi-double; heavily scented.

'Gay Border': white with broad pink border, large, semi-double.

'Gay Sue': white with cream anthers, large, semi-double with frilled petals.

'Gwen Pike': shell-pink, medium, semi-double; compact, bushy growth suitable for container or low border shrub.

'Jean May': shell-pink, large, double; bushy growth.

'Jennifer Susan': pale pink, medium, rose-form double with curled petals.

'Little Pearl': pink buds opening pure white, medium, irregular semi-double.

'Lucinda': pink, medium to large peony form.

'Mignonne': light pink, small, formal double.

'Mine-no-yuki': white, medium, semi-double to loose peony form.

'Misty Moon': light lavender-pink, large, irregular semi-double.

'Narumi-gata': white shaded pink, large, single of cupped form.

'Navajo': rose-red fading to white in centre, large, semi-double.

'Plantation Pink': pink, large, single.

'Queenslander': silvery pink, large, rose-form double; light green foliage; very strong growth.

'Rainbow': white with each petal bordered red, medium to large, single; dense, compact growth.

'Sasanqua Compacta': white with pink edge, medium, single; dwarf plant that makes a beautiful, dense, rounded bush.

'Setsugekka': white, large, semi-double with rippled and fluted petals.

'Silver Dollar': white, medium, peony form.

'Sparkling Burgundy': ruby-rose overlaid with sheen of lavender, small to medium, peony form.

'Sugar Dream': see *C. reticulata* hybrids.

'Taishuhai': white shading to deep red on edge, large, single.

'Tanya': deep rose-pink, single; very slow growth; useful for ground cover, rockery or border.

'Weeping Maiden': white fading to blush-pink at edge, large, single, fragrant.

'White Doves Benten': a sport of 'Mine-no-yuki'; white, informal double; small green and gold leaves.

'Yoi-machi': *C. sasanqua* 'Narumi-gata' x *C. fraterna*; white margined pink, miniature, single; medium, compact, upright growth; E–L.

'Yuletide': orange-red, small, single; compact, upright growth.

Camellia x *williamsii* hybrids

Note: The seed parent in every case is *C. saluenensis* or a *C. saluenensis* hybrid and the pollen parent is a *C. japonica* cultivar.

'Anticipation': NZ, 1962; *C. saluenensis* x *C. japonica* 'Leviathan'; deep rose, large, peony form; upright growth; M.

'Ballet Queen': NZ, 1975; *C. saluenensis* x *C. japonica* 'Leviathan'; salmon-pink, large, peony form; medium growth; M–L.

'Bowen Bryant': Aust., 1960; deep pink, large, semi-double; vigorous, open, upright growth; M.

'Brigadoon': USA, 1960; *C. saluenensis* x *C. japonica* 'Princess Bacciocchi'; rose-pink, medium, semi-double; compact, upright growth; M.

'C. F. Coates': UK, 1935; *C. saluenensis* x *C. japonica* 'Quercifolia'; deep rose, medium, single with fish-tail foliage; open, upright growth; M.

'Caerhays': UK, 1948; *C. saluenensis* x *C. japonica* 'Lady Clare'; rose, medium, semi-double of flat form with three rows of rounded petals and some petaloids mixed with stamens; spreading, pendulous growth.

'China Clay': UK, 1972; *C. saluenensis* x *C. japonica* 'Marjorie Magnificent'; white, medium, semi-double; open growth.

'Daintiness': NZ, 1965; *C. saluenensis* x *C. japonica* 'Hagoromo'; salmon-pink, large, semi-double; medium, open growth; M.

'Debbie': NZ, 1965; *C. saluenensis* x *C. japonica* 'Debutante'; clear spinel-pink, large, peony form; M.

'Donation': UK, 1941; *C. saluenensis* x *C. japonica* 'Donckelaeri'; orchid-pink, large, semi-double; vigorous, compact, upright growth; M.

'Dream Boat': NZ, 1976; *C. saluenensis* x *C. japonica* 'K. Sawada'; bright pink with lavender cast, large, formal double with incurved petals; medium, open, upright growth; M.

'Dresden China': NZ, 1980; *C. saluenensis* x *C. japonica* 'Joshua E. Youtz'; pale pink, large, peony form; slow, spreading, upright growth; M–L.

'E. G. Waterhouse': Aust., 1954; light pink, medium, formal double; vigorous, upright growth; M–L.

'Edward Carlyon': UK, 1981; *C. saluenensis* x *C. japonica* 'Adolphe Audusson'; salmon-pink, medium, rose-form double; spreading growth; M.

'E. T. R. Carlyon': UK, 1972; *C.* x *williamsii* hybrid 'J. C. Williams' x *C. japonica* 'Adolphe Audusson'; candid white, medium, semi-double to rose-form double; vigorous, upright growth.

'Elegant Beauty': NZ, 1962; *C. saluenensis* x *C. japonica* 'Elegans'; deep rose, large, anemone form; open, upright growth; M–L.

'Elsie Jury': NZ, 1964; *C. saluenensis* x *C. japonica* 'Pukekura'; clear medium pink with shaded orchid undertone, large, full peony form; medium, open, spreading growth; M–L.

'Fairy Wand': NZ, 1982; *C. saluenensis* x *C. japonica* 'Fuyajo'; bright rose-red, miniature, semi-double; medium, open, upright growth; M.

'Freedom Bell': USA, 1965; parentage not known; bright red, small, bell-shaped semi-double; vigorous, upright, compact growth, E–M.

'Gay Time': NZ, 1970; *C. saluenensis* x *C. japonica* 'Mathotiana'; white washed and shaded pink, medium, semi-double to formal double; medium, upright growth; M.

'George Blandford': UK, 1958; *C. saluenensis* x *C. japonica* 'Lady Clare'; carmine-rose, large, semi-double to anemone form; vigorous, spreading growth; M.

'Jamie': Aust., 1968; second generation *C.* x *williamsii* hybrid; vivid red, medium, semi-double of hose-in-hose form.

'Jenefer Carlyon': UK, 1972; *C. saluenensis* x *C. japonica* 'C. M. Wilson'; silvery pink, large, semi-double; spreading growth.

'Jury's Yellow': NZ, 1976; *C. saluenensis* hybrid x *C. japonica* 'Gwenneth Morey'; white with cream-yellow petaloids, medium, anemone form; medium, compact, upright growth; E–L.

'Lady Gowrie': Aust., 1954; pink, large, semi-double; vigorous, compact, upright growth; M.

'Margaret Waterhouse': Aust., 1955; light pink, medium, semi-double; vigorous, upright growth; E.

'Mona Jury': NZ, 1976; *C.* x *williamsii* hybrid x *C. japonica* 'Betty Sheffield Supreme'; apricot-pink, large, peony form; medium, open growth; E–L.

'Ruby Bells': NZ, 1987; *C. saluenensis* x *C. japonica* 'Fuyajo'; miniature, single; open, spreading growth; E–M.

'Tregrehan': UK, 1972; *C. saluenensis* x *C. japonica* 'Marjorie Magnificent'; apricot-pink, medium, semi-double to rose-form double; vigorous, upright growth.

'Water Lily': NZ, 1967; *C. saluenensis* x *C. japonica* 'K. Sawada'; lavender tinted bright pink, medium, formal double; vigorous, upright growth; E–M.

'Wilber Foss': NZ, 1971; *C. saluenensis* x *C. japonica* 'Beau Harp'; brilliant pinkish red, large, full peony form; vigorous, upright growth; E–L.

Other hybrids

Refer also to reticulata cultivars, sasanqua cultivars, and *C.* x *williamsii* hybrids.

'Adorable': Aust., 1979; *C. pitardii* seedling; bright pink, medium, formal double; compact, upright growth; M–L.

'Alpen Glo': Aust., 1985; 'Snowdrop' seedling; soft pink, miniature, single flowers with clusters of buds from every leaf axil; green to bronze foliage; quick, upright growth; M–L.

'Angel Wings': USA, 1970; *C. japonica* 'Dr Tinsley' x *C. saluenensis*; white washed and shaded orchid-pink, medium, semi-double with narrow upright petals; medium, compact growth; M.

'Annette Carol': Aust., 1981; *C. pitardii* seedling; pale pink, small, informal double to peony form; tall, open growth; M.

'Ariel's Song': NZ, 1990; *C. fraterna* x *C. tsaii*; white, miniature, single; strong-growing, arching branches; E–L.

'Baby Bear': NZ, 1976; *C. rosiflora* x *C. tsaii*; light pink, miniature, single; dwarf, compact growth; M.

'Baby Willow': NZ, 1983; *C. rosiflora* x *C. tsaii*; white, miniature, single; dwarf, dense, weeping growth; M.

'Bellbird': Aust., 1970; 'Cornish Snow' seedling; pink, small, single; strong, bushy growth; M–L.

'Black Opal': NZ, 1985; *C.* hybrid 'Ruby Bells' x *C. japonica* 'Kuro-tsubaki'; black-red, small to medium, semi-double; slow, compact growth; L.

'Blondy': Aust., 1986; 'Snowdrop' seedling; white, miniature, anemone form; open, upright growth; E–M.

'Buttons 'n Bows': USA, 1985; *C. saluenensis* seedling; light pink shading deeper at edge, small, formal double; medium, compact growth; E–M.

'Christmas Daffodil': USA, 1971; *C. japonica* 'Elizabeth Boardman' x *C.* hybrid 'Tiny Princess'; white tinged blush-pink at petal tips, small, anemone form; vigorous, compact growth; E–M.

'Cinnamon Cindy': USA, 1973; *C. japonica* 'Kenyotai' x *C. lutchuensis*; rose-pink with white centre petaloids, miniature, peony form; strong, slender, upright growth; E–M.

'Contemplation': NZ, 1985; *C. pitardii* x *C. japonica*; lavender-pink, medium, semi-double with occasional petaloids; slow, compact growth; M–L.

'Cornish Snow': England, 1950; *C. saluenensis* x *C. cuspidata*; white with occasional pink blush, small, single; open, upright growth; M.

'Dave's Weeper': pink, small, single; vigorous with long, arching branches; M–L.

'El Dorado': USA, 1967; *C. pitardii* x *C. japonica* 'Tiffany'; light pink, large, full peony form; medium, spreading growth; M.

'Emma Lennard': NZ, 1981; *C. rosiflora* seedling; salmon-pink, miniature, semi-double; medium, open growth; E.

'Fragrant Joy': USA, 1983; *C. japonica* subsp. *rusticana* x *C. lutchuensis*; dark lavender-pink, miniature, rose-form double; medium, upright growth; E–M.

'Fragrant Pink Improved': USA, 1975; *C. japonica* subsp. *rusticana* x *C. lutchuensis*; deep pink, miniature, peony form, fragrant; medium, spreading growth; E–L.

'Garnet Gleam': NZ, 1980; *C. pitardii* seedling; vivid garnet-red with pink filaments and golden stamens, small to medium, trumpet-shaped single; slow, spreading growth; E–L.

'Gay Baby': NZ, 1978; *C. saluenensis* hybrid x *C.* hybrid 'Tiny Princess'; deep orchid-pink, miniature, semi-double; open, upright growth.

'Gay Pixie': Aust., 1979; *C. pitardii* seedling; light orchid-pink with darker pink stripes, large, peony form; open, upright growth; M–L.

'Grace Caple': NZ, 1974; *C. pitardii* x *C. japonica*; faint blush-pink fading to white, large, semi-double to peony form; slow, compact growth; E–L.

'High Fragrance': NZ, 1986; *C. japonica* 'Bertha Harms' x *C.* hybrid 'Scentuous'; pale ivory-pink with deeper pink shading at edge, medium, peony form; vigorous, open growth; M.

'Isaribi': USA, 1981; *C. japonica* 'Berenice Boddy' seedling; rose-pink, miniature, semi-double; vigorous, compact, upright growth; M–L.

'Itty Bit': NZ, 1984; *C. saluenensis* x *C.* hybrid 'Tiny Princess'; soft pink, miniature, anemone form; slow, spreading growth; M.

'Jubilation': NZ, 1978; unnamed *C.* hybrid x *C. japonica* 'Betty Sheffield Supreme'; pink with occasional deeper pink fleck, large to very large, rose-form double; upright growth; M–L.

'Julia Hamiter': USA, 1964; 'Donation' seedling; delicate blush-pink to white, medium, semi-double to rose-form double; medium, compact growth; M.

'Katie Lee': NZ, 1989; *C. japonica* 'Tiffany' x *C. lutchuensis*; light pink deepening at edge, small, single; slow, open growth; M–L.

'Little Lavender': USA, 1965; *C.* hybrid 'Phillipa Forwood' x *C. japonica*; lavender-pink, miniature, anemone form; vigorous, compact, upright growth; M.

'Mary Phoebe Taylor': NZ, 1975; *C. saluenensis* seedling; light rose-pink, very large, peony form; medium, open, upright growth; E–M.

'Minimint': USA, 1970; 'Donation' seedling; white heavily striped pink, small, formal double with high bud centre; slow, bushy growth; M.

'Nicky Crisp': NZ, 1980; *C. pitardii* seedling; pale lavender-pink, large, semi-double; slow, compact growth; E–L.

'Night Rider': NZ, 1985; *C.* hybrid 'Ruby Bells' x *C. japonica* 'Kuro-tsubaki'; very dark black-red, small, semi-double; medium, upright growth; M–L.

'Nonie Haydon': NZ, 1991; *C. pitardii* seedling; pink-rose, medium to large, double; strong growth; M.

'Nymph': NZ, 1982; *C. lutchuensis* x *C. japonica*

'Helen Metson'; pale pink flushed ivory, miniature, semi-double, fragrant; vigorous, spreading growth; E–L.

'Our Betty': USA, 1982; light pink, medium to large, tulip form with two distinct rows of long, slim petals; upright growth; M.

'Our Melissa': Aust., 1986; *C. pitardii* seedling; pink, small, anemone form; vigorous, weeping growth; E–L.

'Persuasion': NZ, 1983; *C. pitardii* x *C. japonica* 'Fuyajo'; purplish red, miniature, single of trumpet shape with golden stamens; slow, spreading growth; E–L.

'Pink Cameo': Aust., 1977; *C. pitardii* seedling; pink overcast silver, medium, peony form; compact, upright growth; M–L.

'Pink Dahlia': USA, 1980; *C. saluenensis* seedling; lavender-pink, small to medium, dahlia-shaped formal double with slender, pointed petals; stiff, bushy growth with long, narrow leaves; L.

'Prudence': NZ, 1971; *C. pitardii* seedling; rich pink, miniature, semi-double; dwarf, upright growth; M.

'Quintessence': NZ, 1985; *C. lutchuensis* hybrid; white with yellow anthers and white filaments, miniature, single, fragrant; slow, spreading growth; E–M.

'Rendezvous': NZ, 1976; *C.* hybrid 'Joyful Bells' x *C. japonica* 'Australis'; scarlet-crimson, medium, semi-double; medium growth; M.

'Rosabelle': Aust., 1981; *C. rosiflora* seedling; rose-pink, miniature, semi-double; spreading, open growth; M.

'Rosiflora Cascade': quite different appearance from *C. rosiflora*; very pale pink, miniature, single; vigorous, weeping growth; pronounced cascading habit; M–L.

'Scented Gem': USA, 1983; *C. lutchuensis* x *C. japonica* 'Tinsie'; fuchsia-pink with white petaloids, miniature, semi-double, fragrant; open, upright growth; M.

'Scentuous': NZ, 1981; *C. japonica* 'Tiffany' x *C. lutchuensis*; white with pink flush on backs of petals, small, semi-double; medium, open growth; M–L.

'Snippet': NZ, 1971; *C. pitardii* seedling; soft pink to almost white centre petals with light pink outer petals, small, semi-double; very slow, bushy growth; M.

'Snowdrop': Aust., 1979; *C. pitardii* x *C. fraterna*; white edged pink, miniature, single; open, upright growth; E–L.

'Spring Festival': USA, 1975; *C. cuspidata* seedling; medium pink fading to light pink in centre, miniature, rose-form double; narrow, upright growth; M–L.

'Spring Mist': USA, 1982; *C. japonica* x *C. lutchuensis*; blush-pink, miniature, semi-double; medium, spreading growth; E–M.

'Sprite': Aust., 1977; *C. pitardii* seedling; light salmon-pink, small, rose-form double; medium, compact, upright growth; M–L.

'Tiny Princess': USA, 1961; *C. japonica* 'Akebono' x *C. fraterna*; white shaded delicate pink, miniature, semi-double to peony form with loose petals and small petaloids; slow growth; E–M.

'Tiny Star': NZ, 1978; *C. japonica* 'Berenice Boddy' x *C.* hybrid 'Tiny Princess'; soft pink, miniature, semi-double; open, upright growth; E–M.

'Tiptoe': Aust., 1965; *C. japonica* x *C.* x *williamsii* 'Farfalla'; silvery pink deepening to cherry-pink, medium, semi-double; compact, upright growth.

'Wirlinga Belle': Aust., 1973; *C. rosiflora* x *C.* x *williamsii* seedling; soft pink, medium, single; medium, open growth; E–M.

'Wirlinga Cascade': Aust., 1987; 'Wirlinga Belle' seedling; pink, miniature, single; vigorous, open, upright growth; M.

'Wirlinga Gem': Aust., 1981; *C.* hybrid 'Tiny Princess' x *C. rosiflora*; pale pink deepening to petal edge, miniature, single; spreading, pendulous growth; E.

'Wirlinga Princess': Aust., 1977; *C.* hybrid 'Tiny Princess' x *C. rosiflora*; pink to white at centre with deeper pink underneath, miniature, single to semi-double; open, spreading growth; M.

APPENDIX 2

Growing camellias under protection

In general, climatic conditions will determine whether protection is necessary for camellias. Frequent extremes of heat or cold, fluctuations in temperature, intense sunshine, strong winds or torrential rain can make protection desirable and, in some climates, essential.

Woodland planting for beauty and for shelter and protection was discussed in chapter 5. In several countries glasshouses, sometimes heated to combat extreme cold, are constructed. The design of glasshouses and their use, with, for example, camellias being moved outside in summer, is a specialist topic, too extensive to be covered here. Anyone considering building one should discuss the possibilities and needs for their district with a local expert.

In New Zealand's favourable climate, a glasshouse is neither necessary nor recommended. Although a shadehouse is not essential either, it can provide added bloom protection or a sheltered working area. Before building a shadehouse, it is important to review the local climate and determine whether such a building is really necessary and how it will be used. The location of the building will be influenced by access, available space, drainage and the proximity of water, as well as aesthetic considerations. If heating is required for a propagation bench, there must be a convenient power source.

As camellia growers have a tendency to expand their hobby, the building should be as large as possible. For container-grown plants, a height of 2 metres (6 feet) will be sufficient, but another metre in height will be necessary if the camellias are to be grown in the ground.

The simplest form of shadehouse is an overhead trellis or frame with shadecloth. The framework can be constructed with treated timber or galvanised-iron piping. Plastic piping may also be used, but there may be a danger of twisting unless strong bracing is attached.

Roof and wall cladding can be either permeable or waterproof. Various grades of shadecloth that allow rain to penetrate are available for protection from sun and wind. Rigid, corrugated-plastic sheets or polythene sheeting are options for waterproof cladding. The shadehouse could be covered in different materials, with shadecloth for three walls and waterproof material on the roof and the side facing the most severe winds and rain.

Wooden battens with spaces between them can be used to make a lath house. The width and thickness of the laths should be adequate to ensure that they are rigid for the length between supporting beams. Over a short distance, they need be no more than 5 x 1 cm (2 x 0.5 in.). The space between the laths will depend upon the intensity of the sun. The hotter the sun, the closer they should be. To give maximum protection, overhead laths should run north-south so the sun moves across them.

The type of floor will depend upon the purpose for which the shadehouse was built. Earth, gravel, bark, 'weedmat' or concrete paving are all options, on their own or in combination. If the camellias are to be planted in the ground, suitable beds with paths between will be needed. Containers can stand on a hard surface or on any of the other materials.

The implications of the design of the shadehouse and the materials used should be considered at every stage of planning. For example, sufficient light and a satisfactory watering programme are essential.

APPENDIX 3

Camellia societies

Addresses of some major societies are:

American Camellia Society, 1 Massee Lane, Fort Valley, Georgia 31030, USA.

Australian Camellia Research Society, 'Moortangi', Mangoplah, NSW 2652, Australia.

International Camellia Society, 10522 Ferncliff Avenue, Baton Rouge, Louisiana 70815, USA.

New Zealand Camellia Society, PO Box 204, Whanganui, New Zealand.

The Royal Horticultural Society, Rhododendron and Camellia Committee, 80 Vincent Square, London SW1P 2PE, England.

Southern California Camellia Society, 3230 Mesaloa Lane, Pasadena, California 91107, USA.

Membership representatives of the International Camellia Society who would be willing to provide information about the ICS or local camellia societies are:

Africa: Mr Leslie Riggall, Fern Valley, Igwababa Road, Kloof 3600, Natal, South Africa.

Asia: Mr Hiroshi Tsushi, 33F Sunshine Building, 3-1-1, Higashi Ikeburkuro, Toshima-Ku, Tokyo 170, Japan.

Australia: Miss N. J. Swanson, 43 Wellington Road, East Lindfield, NSW 2070, Australia.

France: M. Claude Thoby, Levieux Grand Chemin, Route de Paris, 44470 Carquefou, France.

Germany: Dr Klaus Hacklander, Simeonstrasse 5, D55oo, Trier, Germany.

Italy: Arch. Franco Giorgetta, Via Fiori Chiari, 8-20i2i, Milano, Italy.

New Zealand: Mr R. H. Clere, 8 Chesham Avenue, Taupo, New Zealand.

Portugal: Senhora Clara de Seabra, Praceta Prof. Egas Moniz, 167-4Esq 4100 Porto, Portugal.

Spain: Don Juan Armada Diez de Rivera, Avda Doctor Arce 4, 28002, Madrid, Spain.

United Kingdom & Isle of Man: Mr H. C. Short, 41 Galveston Road, East Putney, London SW15 2RZ, United Kingdom.

Channel Islands & Republic of Ireland with Belgium, Denmark, Finland, Malta, Netherlands and other regions: Mrs Ann Bushnell, Lower Hall, Rue de la Pompe, Augres, Trinity, Jersey, Channel Islands.

United States: Mrs Edith Mazzei, 1486 Yosemite Circle, Clayton, California 94517, USA.

APPENDIX 4

Exhibiting camellias

For many people, exhibiting competitively can add to the pleasure of growing camellias. Even a novice can produce a champion bloom. The first time is probably the most difficult, whether it is at a local garden club show or a national camellia society event. There is a lot to be learned by talking to other exhibitors. If you happen to produce a champion bloom, the others will all want your advice. These brief notes are designed to help those who are new to exhibiting camellias.

1. Read the show rules carefully. Note the requirements for leaves and naming of blooms.

2. When selecting a bloom, consider carefully the class in which it is to be entered. It should be fresh, undamaged, and of a form, colour and size typical of the variety.

3. Take great care in picking and handling blooms, one at a time, to avoid any damage. This can be done two or three days before the show and the blooms kept in a vase or small container in a cool place. Young blooms will develop to perfection in this time. Ensure that blooms do not rub against each other. Bruising must be avoided. Ensure also that each bloom is labelled correctly.

4. Take care transporting blooms to the show. Use containers with lids, deep enough to allow space between the blooms and the closed lid. If cardboard boxes are to be used, cover the bottom with plastic sheeting, then add some layers of damp newspaper, and finish with dampened, shredded paper or sphagnum moss.

5. Pack the blooms with great care. Place them one at a time, using loose packing to hold each one firm. Keep them spaced sufficiently to avoid bruising. More experienced exhibitors have their own systems of grouping different blooms in separate, labelled boxes to make things easier at the show.

6. Keep the boxes flat in the car and out of the sun, with lids on, until it is time to display the blooms.

7. Winning blooms are invariably well presented. Remember to work with one bloom at a time and avoid any damage to it. Even loose clothes brushing against a bloom can cause bruising. Arrange the bloom to sit easily in the container provided, facing the front, so that it can be seen to perfection. A fine but light spray of water may help to maintain freshness.

8. Some cultivars produce award-winning blooms time and again. 'Dr Clifford Parks', 'Pavlova', 'Lila Naff', 'Harold L. Paige', 'Elegans Supreme', 'Elegans Champagne', 'Tiffany', 'Easter Morn', 'Wildfire', and 'Twilight' are regular top performers, but there are hundreds of others.

Bibliography

Anderson, E. B., *Camellias*, Blandford Press, London, 1961.

Anon., *Bonsai: Culture and Care of Miniature Trees*, Sunset Books, California, 1977.

—*Camellias as a Hobby*, Oregon Camellia Society, 1949.

—*Camellia Culture*, New Zealand Camellia Society Handbook, 1970, 1981.

—*Camellia Culture in Queensland*, Queensland Camellia Society, 1986.

—*Camellias Illustrated and How to Grow Them*, Oregon Camellia Society, 1958.

—*Camellias*, Efford Experimental Horticulture Station, UK, Leaflet no. 7, 1970–1982.

—*Successful Camellia Growing*, Victorian Branch, Australian Camellia Research Society.

Bieleski, Val (ed.), *Growing Better Camellias in the 1990s*, New Zealand Camellia Society Handbook, 1991.

Bliss, Amelia and Carey, S., *Camellias: The Huntingdon Gardens*, The Huntington Library, California.

Chan, Peter, *The Complete Book of Bonsai*, Bracken Books, London, 1989.

Chang Hung Ta and Bartholomew, Bruce, *Camellias*, Timber Press, Portland, Oregon, 1984.

Chidiamian, Claude, *Camellias for Everyone*, Doubleday, New York, 1959.

Donnan, William J., *Beautiful Camellias of Descanso Gardens*, Southern California Camellia Society.

Durrant, Tom, *The Basic Care of Camellias*, New Zealand Camellia Society Handbook, 1986.

—*The Camellia Story*, Heinemann, Auckland, 1982.

Feathers, D. L. and Brown, M. H.(eds.), *The Camellia: Its History, Culture and Genetics*, American Camellia Society, 1978.

Feng Guomei, Xia Lifang and Zhu Xianghong, *Yunnan Camellias*, Science Press, Beijing, 1986.

Haydon, Neville, Camellia Haven (Takanini, New Zealand) catalogues, 1989, 1990, 1991.

Hume, Harold H., *Camellias in America*, 2nd ed., McFarland, Pennsylvania, 1955.

Kincaid, Mrs Paul, *The Camellia Treasury*, Hearthside Press, New York, 1964.

Koreshoff, Dorothy and Vita, *Bonsai in New Zealand*, Boolarong Publications, Brisbane, 1987.

Longhurst, Peter and Savige, T. J., *The Camellia*, Bay Books, Sydney, 1982.

Macoboy, Stirling, *The Colour Dictionary of Camellias*, Lansdowne Press, Sydney, 1981.

Savell, Bob and Andrews, Stan, *Growing Camellias in Australia and New Zealand*, Kangaroo Press, Kenthurst, Australia, 1982.

Sealy, J. Robert, *A Revision of the Genus Camellia*, The Royal Horticultural Society, London, 1958.

Simpson, A. G. W., *Camellias: Their Colourful Kin and Friends*, Murray Publishers, New South Wales, 1978.

Tourje, E. C. (ed.), *Camellia Culture*, MacMillan, New York, 1958.

Trehane, David, *A Plantsman's Guide to Camellias*, Ward Lock, London, 1990.

—*Camellias*, Wisley Handbook 37, Royal Horticultural Society, 1980.

Urquhart, Beryl Leslie, *The Camellia*, vols. I & II, Leslie Urquhart Press, 1956–60.

Wang Jiaxi and Ma Yue, *China's Rare Flowers*, Morning Glory Press, Beijing, 1986.

Webber, Leonard, *Bonsai for the Home and Garden*, Angus and Robertson, Australia, 1989.

Yu Dejun (chief compiler), *Botanical Gardens of China*, Science Press, Beijing, 1983.

The following periodicals are issued to members by the Camellia Societies indicated:

American Camellia Society:
The American Camellia Year Book (annual)
The Camellia Journal (quarterly)

Australian Camellia Research Society:
Camellia News (quarterly)

International Camellia Society:
International Camellia Journal (annual)

New Zealand Camellia Society:
New Zealand Camellia Bulletin (three times a year)

Southern California Camellia Society:
Camellia Nomenclature triennial
Camellia Review (quarterly)

Index

Illustrations are indicated by bold numerals.